The Light Most Glad of All

The Light Most Glad of All

Poems by

Ken Meisel

© 2023 Ken Meisel. All rights reserved.
This material may not be reproduced in any form, published, reprinted,
recorded, performed, broadcast,
rewritten or redistributed without
the explicit permission of Ken Meisel.
All such actions are strictly prohibited by law.

Cover photo by Ken Meisel
Author photo by Anita Scott-Meisel
Cover design by Shay Culligan

ISBN: 978-1-63980-379-8

Kelsay Books
502 South 1040 East, A-119
American Fork, Utah 84003
Kelsaybooks.com

For Anita, since always and for always

"I summon you to the frosted almond tree
to the winged souls of roses;
we have so many things we have to talk about,
you, my companion, companion of my soul."

—Miguel Hernandez, *Elegy*

Acknowledgments

Thank you to the following publications, where versions of these poems previously appeared:

12 Mile Review: "The Lords of Shouting Unravel Her & Me in Light"
Backchannels: "Sunday Morning Prayer"
The Big Windows Review: "Wound Healing"
Concho River Review: "The Light Most Glad of All," "Coma"
Crab Creek Review: "Book of Love"
I-70 Review: "Her," "Punk," "The Angel w/ a Winterberry in its Hand," "Marriage"
January Review: "Quick Postcard (The Angel of the Ravel District, Barcelona)"
Kentucky Review: "Our Lady of the Rosary"
The MacGuffin: "Love's Body"
Muddy River Poetry Review: "The Angel of Yearning Speaks to Me," "In the Almond Groves, Highway 5, San Joaquin Valley," "A Stage Play Exposition on Love & Marriage"
Rabid Oak: "The Angel Ashriel Lifts Me Out of Me," "Confession"
San Pedro River Review: Stanza one of "Wedding Ceremony in Battery Park, Charleston, S.C."
Scapegoat Review: "Delight"
Sheila-Na-Gig: "Contemplation in a Small City Park w/ Apricot Trees," "One Holy Night, Santa Fe, New Mexico"
St. Katherine Review: "Coma, Awakening," "Orb, Floating in the Almond Groves," "Love," "Parable w/ a Girl-Woman Petting an Injured Cat Before I Knew Her Inside the Coma Awakening of Time"
Trampoline Magazine: "Contemplation on Covetousness & Love"

"Contemplation in a Small City Park w/ Apricot Trees" was awarded Editor's Choice Award in *Sheila-Na-Gig,* Volume # 7.1. (2022)

"Her" was nominated for a Pushcart Prize by *I-70 Review.*

"Contemplation in a Small City Park w / Apricot Trees" was nominated for a Pushcart Prize by *Sheila-Na-Gig.*

Contents

Preface, Forward & Prologue on the Gazer Within 15

Coma, Awakening

Coma 19
Orb, Floating in the Almond Groves 23
Midsummer's Madness When I Met My Baby 26
Coma, Awakening 27
The Lords of Shouting Unravel Her & Me
 in Light 29
Wedding Ceremony in Battery Park,
 Charleston, S.C. 35
Marriage 40
Parable w/ a Girl-Woman Petting an Injured Cat
 Before I Knew Her Inside the Coma
 Awakening of Time 42
A Stage Play Exposition on Love & Marriage 46

Book of Love

Book of Love 51
Jeqon, The Inciter Angel (Echo Park) 55
Monique Jean 60
Lucille Marie Jean 62
Punk 63
Contemplation on Covetousness & Love 65
The Angel of Yearning Speaks to Me 67

In the Almond Groves

Confession 77
Love 80
Wound Healing 81
Delight 83
In the Almond Groves, Highway 5,
 San Joaquin Valley 84

Love's Body	86
Quick Postcard	
(The Angel of the Ravel District, Barcelona)	87
Sunday Morning Prayer	90
Contemplation in a Small City Park	
w/ Apricot Trees	92

The Light Most Glad of All

Our Lady of the Rosary	99
The Archangel Jophiel, Laying Down	
on the Blanket w/Me	101
One Holy Night, Santa Fe, New Mexico	113
The Angel Ashriel Lifts Me Out of Me	115
The Angel with a Winterberry in its Hand	119
Her	121
The Light Most Glad of All	123
Coda: Afterwards	126

Preface, Forward & Prologue on the Gazer Within

"Then all at once the messenger was there, amid the simmer of wedding guests"
—Rilke, *Alcestis*

The bride & groom were upstairs at the summer inn
& just seeking a little quiet time, a little peace for
themselves before they joined the guests down below
again, for the rest of the party; for dinner & dancing.
& the couple was standing together on a simple balcony
that overlooked the high cliff where the sea below
roiled & raged & hurled itself against the mantel rock,
& they noticed the sky was thick with white feathers
while the wedding guests mingled, toasted & danced,
& outpaced, in their excitement, the world of the dead.
The bagpiper played more steadily now—just for fun—
& below them, they could hear the raucous revelry
of the wedding ceremony as it took on a life of its own
like the whole labyrinth of the world, or like the reality
of an eternal wandering that joins people together & / or
separates them, only to join them in other places, again.
& then—all at once—the messenger was there, amid the
simmer of wedding guests. & there was a sudden stillness,
& an intimacy so that, when the bride & groom looked
down, trying to see what had silenced everything,
all they saw was a lone figure walking down a path
between the guests & he was just softly, gently, touching
folks on the shoulder, the wrist, even on the reddened mouth,
& all the guests stopped, & they gazed at one another
like they were in the original Eden, but not as sinners
& not even as pairs but, in fact, as selves curled up in shells,
or like turtles—just men & women in tuxedos, gowns,
& the messenger's soft touch—each time it occurred—
unfurled someone from a kind of armor or a fistedness,
& the eternal ones of the dream, all the awakened ones,
paused & one-by-one, gazed deeply into stunned eyes
as if trying to see—by purely hallucinatory means—
all the other lifetimes trying right now at this wedding—
like seeds—to be born. & suddenly the messenger was
upstairs with the couple, holding them tight & *in* them,
like some impressive mystery flame or lantern light,

& what happened next was a downpour of snow-white
almond blossoms falling like a wedding dress all over
the couple so that they were not at birth at all but—in fact—
at conception; & they were flames to one another; asleep
& dreaming. & there was a stillness where the couple
saw themselves falling into comas & dissipating in the sun
so that the wind—like a milk crate man—whisked them
away . . . into the double dream where rebirth & love
originate. & then something dark wove itself around
the balcony, like it was snake stirred by envy. & it
felt so good, except that its aim was to creep over
the messenger, there in the couple, & blind it.
& it named its dark woven scarf *culture*. & all it did
was chase its own amphetamine tail, like a delirious
hyper-active monkey, inside a tree of its own making.
& something alive & vibrant fell away then, into dullness,
into a mistrust and canceling out of one another,
& just before the couple went to sleep, the messenger
whispered that love is the awakening of the Eternal
Gazer within. & that without the Gazer, we would
see one another through the dark pall of reluctance—
like a fear of being born: & only gazing love reveals,
& only through a light most glad of all, will we ever see.

Coma, Awakening

"... and we are two ghosts who search and find each other from afar."

—Miguel Hernandez, *Love Ascended Between Us*

Coma

On the curtain of the old house on the corner, a fly
roams upward & downward on it, like an irritation

trying to find its source. Someone's put a kettle on,
& its wheezing screams go uninterrupted & a cat

on the chair just looks up, following the fly with its
green, cocktail eyes—& that's just the prop in the poem

to alert you to the fact that it's my old house. & I'm
no longer living there because I've left it, I'm divorced.

& the cat was lost to me in the divorce &, likewise,
the kettle & the kitchen &, when I put the coin in the slot

to see the naked lady there, I'd been divorced just two hours
& my trousers fell heavy over my old leather shoes

the color of flathead catfish, & my wristwatch read 2pm,
& I was hung over, but aware enough to know who I

saw in the small oval shape as she posed & stretched
her arms up over her dark hair that was shaped into

a stylish bun. & I saw her pouring herself into a coma
& that her eyes, like a small mouth bass's eyes,

were hysterical & full of dark water persuasion.
& in those days dating was like going to torpid sleep

only to awaken in a brothel house, meeting a woman
who resembled a fish wrapped in a shawl & with pearl

earrings & eyes that called, or spoke to you about what
your dreams couldn't even express or crash into &, after

I put another coin in the slot, I saw the special one
who'd bring me her collision & she wasn't naked

or in the business but somehow just daubed the edge
of the oval room where the other posing woman was,

& this woman had eyes the color of blue ash & a smile
like a forgery & so I knew she was the one for me. &

she was what the fresh morning-after refers to as holy, & I
could see that she moved in a way that foreshortened time,

& that before she entered the small, pornographic oval,
she'd spent a month of days making jewelry in the almond

orchards. & some women spend a bicycle's worth of days
as angels-in-training; they're made of a fractional rendering

& so they take their time with everything & that's how
they love within the light most glad of all, like diamond light.

& isn't it like that, that when you're transfixed by one lady
the other one comes along . . . ? & this was in Amsterdam, years

ago & not even in the city I bought a house in, & the fly
on the curtain roamed up, down, like childhood, & I awoke,

alone there. & I walked the lonely canals, looking in vain
for her in the way one would troll a fish with a fishing pole.

& recurring images are what love's made of . . . & images
correct the lovers trying to discover one another—in truth—

like they're trying to awaken from a deep, dark lime blue
sleep, or like they've just been in a coma, waiting for each

other in the exact way the man selling soft brioche buns waits
for the dolorous pigeons to drunkenly scatter under him—

like voiceless, muttering dream fragment birds made of coal
& iridescent slices of someone's green feathered coat material—

so he can toss the scraps to them & tell himself they're birds
infused by chocolate. & love is a deep dream, it's a backslide

in the same exact way its made most definitely of a light
most glad of all & so it renders us comatose & awake

so we can know ourselves in the theater of the dream—
awakening itself from old lines of poetry written a long time ago.

Or maybe it freshens in the same exact way that the blind girl
juggling outside the music box store waits on time for me

so I can stop & tell her what time the church clock says
& tell her, likewise, that her face is a fugitive saffron yellow,

& composed of the same exact music that makes swallows
suddenly scatter away from the ringing church bells.

& maybe tell her everything we dream about—all of it—
is the light most glad of all, composing all we see.

& years later, when I stopped at a stylish little café for an aperitif,
the woman that brought me the drink, just a dubonnet,

had the same exact blue ash eyes & a forgery smile & I fell into
the ointment of that coma, until this light most glad of all

caressed me into a book I was reading so I could forget it—
for maybe eighty years—& then awaken in it, just like this . . .

& find myself in Paris, France, no less, seeking the one who'd
be my fortune & my walking companion for the years,

& maybe see the old man & his violet wife sitting there
at the café, holding hands together, bathed in lemon light,

& then maybe, afterwards, I could search the oval again—
in that pornographic little coin slot room where the ages pass

over the open graves like perfumed luminescent wings—
to where the woman in the almond orchards goes on her

evening strolls looking left & right through those opaque
misted flowers, for someone old & young, like me.

Orb, Floating in the Almond Groves

Off Highway 5, in the San Joaquin Valley, I spotted a gold finch, his
yellow shoulders prideful, glorious, like poured stars,

& he was singing in the almond groves.
Let me whisper a secret to you: I heard the bird

before I saw it. I'd been kneeling in the orchards,
trying to pray. & that is because prayer

is the way we try to complete something. & I was
finished with something lonesome in me,

but they never tell you that in church. They tell you
that prayer opens possibility—which might be true—

but prayer
is actually asking death to move a life aside

      &

when I was praying like this I'd never been
to California
much less the San Joaquin Valley

      &

the sadness of it all made me believe some people are born
by contradictory value & others, by veneration,

& I wanted that. I wanted the veneration.

      &

I mattered so little to what my name told me about me
& so I started to pray,
just at the edge of some revolt.

      & the way

the almond blossoms fell to the ground, so soft & silent
        like angel fingerprints

trying, one at a time, to kiss the sore spots of the earth,
        captured me, moved me inward.

& that they could smell of honey, against the dry ground
& love a limitlessness in them anyway . . . & do a duty in order to love
        a perfection in them even as they dropped

without the slightest prompting, made the softest turning
        of faith rise me.

        & something let go then, in me.
& I could see, without a shape, someone shrouded & veiled
        in the distant white canopy

where the white petals were falling like a Universe being born
& I couldn't fully see her there—a light most glad of all—

but she was there, waiting in that way we anticipate a dream
to launch again—to revive its cinematic pictures for us.

        &

incarnation is so unintelligible at first, it's so un-invented,

        &

the mind can't *find* it . . . & it's never our two eyes that are first to see,
but it's just the *wound* in us—so long & so patient in the waiting—

        &

the one who gains the wound to love can only find it
        through veneration—I swear that's true—
            & through someone else
        who *opens* likewise . . .

        & so . . .

I could *sense* her there, like a flickering orb,
opening like a star in the Universe

    & so

I waited, in an inexpressible anticipation, like I was a branch
of extended almond blossoms that had been told they'd shiver

      & fall till I was emptied,

        & then I'd be ready to be seized by something
        miraculous.

& the unctuous little rat there, hunched & twitching
& grinning at me by a hot spot under the moon, waited . . .

      it waited for me—oh I swear it did—till I was done praying.

    &

it kept me whole & attentive, till that orb came. & I saw.

Midsummer's Madness When I Met My Baby

I couldn't do it all again, what with the summer roses.
I'd wanted to be single; an unattached man free to pursue

the tulip mania of the reckless bars & the dance clubs
where the waifs & strays & the wages of sin fed into the waters

of providence. & I'd been praying for something special
to come to me in the orchards; & it was veneration that'd

led me to walk *not* in the public ways. & Ursa Minor,
with its circular sweep through the dog's tail of the sky,

swept all the other stars & almond blossoms away so that,
alone, all by myself, I could see the strongest star among

all the rest; & then, sit there & watch it do its Vitus dance,
its dancing mania, until the morning depressed the bright sky gray,

& the walkers, seeking their coffee, arrived by foot.
But, when she stepped down the path, walking over the

wandering wood & shouldering her small purse over her
left shoulder like she was managing her shadow, her

after-glow, &, when she tossed her hair above her eyes so that
she could see who I was, so suddenly, to her, I dreamed

she was one of the tuneful nine, those muses that join
a man on a walkway just as he's aiming to step away

from himself. & she was dressed in short pants & a
summer top, & hoop earrings & red lipstick—it was the 80s—

& some small part of me saw her as a flower, something
pollinized. & she was history & music & elegy, & epic

& lyric poetry & tragedy, & comedy & astrology & dancing,
& I knew she was a madness most hypnotic, & all mine.

Coma, Awakening

When the dream awakens & the sleeping coma
is no longer present, the self finds an awakening—

its love revelation—in the other. & maybe all this
happens at a simple restaurant & the couple is

serving one another a hot dish of something
& she's there, pouring him his wine & he's

smiling, receiving it, & now they are feeding
one another spoons of food, & suddenly he's

looking intently into her eyes, just to see her;
& what he sees then, also, is himself, what he's

meant to be to himself & to her & to them,
as if the future, that open water, is here; & time

is the cellophane boundary that is pierced.
& the coma is just the remembering of the other

right now as the other that was always inevitable.
& maybe love is that portal. & so the couple

preserves it, that portal; & they build an entire
world inside it, so they can always move

through it, like dance steps down a dancehall.
&, just what *is* the coma, awakening, if not

just this remembrance of one another, inside
the cellophane boundary that time has pierced?

She said to me: "let's stay young inside this,
forever." Wasn't that the first vow? & I said—

& just with my eyes because I didn't have the
words for it yet—" it is a fervor that gives its

self to another so that what was once solid,
becomes porous & a makeshift for another's

life." & didn't Gilbert say, in one of his poems,
that the spirit—inside the self—is, in fact,

something voiceless flying lovely, over
an empty landscape? Yes, her eyes said back

to me, that is what love is: "it is the coma,
awakened, that the lover flies so emptied

over a lovely landscape, into the homestead
of another."

The Lords of Shouting Unravel Her & Me in Light

1

It was pretty late in the afternoon, Labor Day weekend,
the ramshackle parade, pulsing down Joseph Campau.
I remember, as I gazed down at the street from my window,
that too many men had been drinking—probably beer—

& probably they'd been drinking since early in the morning

as the sly, drunken boat sunrise
had wobbled and climbed through the rough spindly trees
that were lining the street year after dogged year

& I remember that, as the parade drifted past me,
dense with parade floats & young women riding rear-seat
in gaudy convertibles & waving at us

that one of the drunken men had started swinging at a float's
Woody Wood Pecker head

& he kept missing it so
he'd curse & he'd cuss

as he took another faulty aim at it, & I remember
that the gaiety, the revelry, the raucous celebration

going on
felt, somehow, just at the edge of becoming violent

2

"& love, you know, is a relentless uncovering of everything
we're afraid of," she said—

"it's like we're feathered in fear—like a piñata, or a costume—
some being caught & squirming in the light hourglass of time—

& love, the interaction of it, strips us naked to ourselves
& we're revealed as to what we were once afraid of

&, afraid, we risk anyway . . .
& we lose, bit by discovered bit, any temptation for violence . . .

3

& it's so in-woven in us, and we're inseparable from it, *love* . . ."

& she'd hum to me as we lay there watching the sunset
& she'd curl up next me as I took turns playing a ukulele

as the night fell hard over the rough buildings of the city
& she'd turn over and request that I strum the Bee Gees

song, "To Love Somebody," & I'd sing, "I want my life to be
lived with you, lived with you:"

& she'd sit straight up, her vireo's eyes straight on me,
& she'd kiss me hard,

her left hand, stretching behind her, clutching the air.

4

I live and breathe for you, is what the song claimed,

& as the Labor Day parade bellowed on—horns, drums, dancers,
drunks, everyone—I want to confess to you that

as it rambled past me, heading to the city's farther border,
nobody in the shit-wood-flat we were living in noticed

the fire being set to the back stairs—it was set by two men
getting revenge on the land lady—

&, in our hurried panic to get the hell out of there

we never noticed that a girl, someone's babysitter, just a girl of 14 was assaulted on the stairway leading up

to our flat

5

& the song said, "and in my brain I'll see your face again . . ."

6

& in my brain I'll see your face again

is what we think to ourselves when the avenging angels

clash with

the providing angels—

those angels who carry forward all our memories & all our duties

especially those memories that are cut like mirrors when we least expect it—

&, afterwards, after the clash's storms of reverie, melancholy, awe,

we wake up the next morning—so flush with homesickness

& the fluttering faces of those we quake to remember—

& we say to ourselves, "& in my brain, I'll see your face again"

& so the girl of 14, someone's baby sitter, is probably fifty years old now

&, at her dinner table, she's thinking, "is my body just an edible pear?
even my husband's lips on me feel insatiable, hungry,"

& when he strolls home, tired, a day plumber, he stops at her,
squints, asks what's for dinner & he gently kisses her, lifts her face

to the light

& the old dog runs up to them, tail wagging, & the woman, fifty,
thinks to herself, "it's not so bad, this must be the happy time,

the love light,
this must be what all my days from then till now are made of—"

8

& you know when we kissed, lathered up in a bathtub, years ago
in my apartment, a bottle of May wine beside us

& her adventurous lover's mouth all over mine—
it's my wife I'm now speaking of—

I told her
I never wanted to be in that burning city again

where even an annual Labor Day Parade
could turn violent and fiery, & a girl
could find herself manhandled by a drunken stranger;

& my wife looked hard into me, seeking why it was I'd let this
sweet moment be ruined or spoiled between us
by some other violent narration in my brain—

some trespass or some interruption, so unforgettable—

                        & I turned myself over to her,

I let my wet featherless body
slip inside her arms as we soaked in that bathtub

& I said to her, "I want my life to be lived with you,
lived with you . . ."

& she whispered in my right ear,
my face beside hers—there, in that claw foot bathtub—

that love portends the greater of us; it requires of us a duty
to live beyond who we are & beyond what's made us

                &,

on the next morning, at dawn, you know it was so very strange
that down near the freeway lanes, as we ruffled through our burned flat,

we heard this strange odd bawling & yelping . . .

& it was the Lords of Shouting, those angel masters of howling

that God assigned to sing awake the blessed first light of dawn . . .

& one of them, a body made of rough torn rags & feathers
came bawling up at me like a wing torn from some larger, grander bird,
& the one assigned Lord of Shouting hailed me, it shouted to me,

"we are torn feathers made of all this undressing . . . we are relentlessly

                naked—

we are relentlessly naked & we bathe & sing in this pink veil

                of morning clouds—

& we sing until the sun rises over the haggard trees, the tired cities . . .
& the lovers relentlessly empty themselves of fear;

    we sing until the lovers strip naked
    to the light most glad of all

& they rid themselves of any inclination of violence . . .

    & we keep on singing for them

until one-by-one they become feathered in this pink eternal light;
& by and through the soft will
of surrendering themselves to their untold beauty
     & to their vulnerability to precious things

they learn the loving of another's light is salvation's bargain:
it's the way we move the love-light of each other's souls along . . ."

    9

"& we sing your love lights awake! We sing for every loving gift
you offer to an innocent life not yours; it's for all of that, we sing."

Wedding Ceremony in Battery Park, Charleston, S.C.

1

The eyes are the gates to the everything, says the Angel of Light

    to the opened ears of the young couple standing in front
    of the reverend and speaking their wedding vows softly

to each other, here at this wedding ceremony in Battery Park,
in Charleston, South Carolina—amidst a sprawling cathedral

of live oak trees and wedding angels perched in a clerestory
    of tree branches.

The spires of churches explode hymns into the dopamine heat.

    And there is a broken harp string in each of us too—
    says the Angel of Melody to the young couple.

And plucking it unlocks the gate to the lover's code

    that makes one person walk one hundred rivers

to another person's door.

2

So the bride and groom take hold of each other's hands firmly—

like they are wading through an incoming tidal wave into each

other's eyes while along Broad Street, a parade wiggles through

lacquered heat.

3

The wedding angels have great big eyes on their feathery wings
and they wear pearls across their toes. They gather and sprawl

like bromheadia orchids in the tangle of live oak branches
and allamanda vines. They stick like glue in transistor radios.

They happen to be cousins to the southern swallowtail
and the cloudless sulfur—those flirtatious angelic butterflies.

They sheathe in a membrane of music that confounds
the fluttering soul as it wafts through heat past the colonials

of Rainbow Row to this altar, where the young couple
steps forward, vows in hand, so as to seal their nuptials

and ruffle their young innocent lives like gooseflesh.

The wedding angels dance on the fluttering eyelids of people
    getting married, and they come alive when we're vulnerable.

God unfurls angels from the broken harp string of eyelashes
        like hallucinatory butterflies—

and they fly free in order to open all the lover's gates.

They awaken only when we—with our eyes—blink the gates open . . .

The lover's gates are shimmering moments of playful glee that,
    during joy, we slip into each other's wide alive hearts—

so says the Angel of Corpuscle to me. And the angel insists

4

that *marriage* is just a vibrating biosphere of improvisational energy—
which is God's musical field of rhythm and blues.

It's the rumba of elation into the bones, and back.

Improvising with one another is just the first step on the road
    to capturing love's exhilaration, so says the Angel of Initiation

to the young bride as she leans forward to twirl the wedding ring
around her groom's left finger while he stands upright—
    across from her—his neck jutting out like an engrossed crane.
Now the wedding rings ignite like stars on the couple's fingers.

And God showers the big bang into the bride and groom's eyes.

5

Now God tells the bride and groom
that we're made of broken harp strings and blooming zodiacs—
    our bodies are formed in anguish and hope—
    this is the exultant manner by which we arrive together.

And God instructs the young couple that we must open
    our eyes wide to each other—as wide as holy temples—

and we must do so with open hearts of improvisational risk,

which is what the lovers Romeo and Juliet did one night

    in order to open all their chakra gates
    which is both tragic and wondrous:

    it's both impetuous and intentional:

    and it's the Inscription in the Book of Love
    that this couple is writing for themselves today.

So says the Angel of Interlude, the Angel of Intermezzo, and the Angel of Design. So say the Three Fates that guide us into nuptial.

The opened chakra gates unlock the *5th world* of Human Beings—

    which is the Age of Aquarius and the stump of a tree
    blown apart. It is the age of Expansion. It's the age of Spirit.

And all the guests who rise in light, step forward to witness.

6

Now the couple bends in to kiss each other, their eyes widen open,
which is an erotic fandango up a sound wave antenna—

and one of the gates blasts open from above the tree canopy:

and a tangle of wedding angels and swallowtail butterflies

parachutes around the embracing young couple—smothering them—
and the guests celebrate by tossing strings of confetti . . .

    Love is an anthropomorphic type of density first.
    It's tight, and we think of it as human; it isn't tho—
    Love's just trapped light, bound in a spun cocoon.

    Then it's an entwined rope of tight fear uncoiling—
    and then it's a rhythm of erotic invention. *For years.*

    Afterwards, at a funeral, it's a smell of lilies in the air—
    it's the aroma is sweet cane sugar, stuck in the nose—

    so says the Angel of Lament, slipping down the trunk
    of an oak tree to greet the couple clasping fingers together.

    . . . Love and *Death dance in the gooseflesh.*
    The Wedding Angels rule all the octaves we sing.

    So says the Angel of Eternal Song inside the clanging bells.

7

Now God whispers to the bride and groom that the act of gazing

into each other's eyes is the Obligation Seal we'll use to affirm
        and signify each other:

it's an extremely strange act we'll do—it alienates us forever—

so says the Angel of Mystery to me and to the reader who is now
reading this poem—while it joins us together, simultaneously—

and it agitates and matriculates our homesickness, which is *love*.

8

And making love with each other plucks the broken harp string
that unlocks the mystery of why we walk rivers to find each other

in the first place—so says God to the wind, jitterbugging in the fields.

So says the Angel of Melody, with its successive wing bursts of sound,
and The Angel of Hope, to the jubilant birds whistling in the trees.

And this improvisational lovemaking we all engage in—

    (which is what this couple will do later on in a quiet room
    while on a radio a song called the *Unchained Melody* plays . . .
which is—dear reader—a love song packed dense with wedding angels
and an inextricable glue that's part intention, part surrender,
    part quivering-energy-field and part spirit-octave on fire—)

is exactly what this poem, this wedding ceremony, is all about:

and it's a part so obvious
as to be one man and one woman arriving here together

at long last to claim it, to love it big as life, to finish it.

Marriage

> "By it I must go to you, love so securely hidden"
> —J Ramon Jimenez

There were six invited guests: the past, the future,
& the present, & we were there too, she & I, us,
standing there, waiting for the bagpipes to begin.
& I swear the wedding seemed like a big wiggling fish,
but I won't get into that &, besides, most weddings
begin as hallucinations & end up as poetry, or
maybe as country music songs gone sour or divine,
& I all I remember, as I watched her walking
toward me, was not just that she was as exotically
enthralling as a capricious swan's feather coughed out
of girlhood but that, in the end, I'd never know
the all of her—the full entirety of her that would
hold herself alive & so utterly irresistible in one face
as she traced the lipstick over her lips & sprayed
that fragrance all over her neck so as to disguise herself
some more from me so I'd have to endlessly
seek her—& that, alone, created such a deep, homesick
hunger in me that I felt suddenly a bit sick for the
deep want of it &, maybe too, a little bit grateful,
you know, for the full chance to try for it, for the full
reach for it, you know. & I think that when she saw me,
she recognized that she'd already seen me spying
on her through a peep hole & through a hunter's
canticle of years till now as she roamed, like a lone
star orb, counting all the white blossoms as they fell
through the thick-floored almond orchards of eternity
while I frolicked in the murmuring wind. & that,
in the end, the peep hole is really just a mirror
where we can see one another until all the waiting
time is over. &, you know, love's a reflecting
mirror where the six guests weave in & out. & it's
a peep hole where the spy & the spied upon
change positions, over & over, until they can't
lose one another anymore, & so the ceremony
of marriage is an ordeal of hide & seek, of seek

& find through a peep hole & mirror, till the end,
& then it's an empty mirror the two walk through,
like star orbs into an almond orchard grove
where the petals are peep holes, all over again.

Parable w/ a Girl-Woman Petting an Injured Cat Before I Knew Her Inside the Coma Awakening of Time

When we were fighting, just after the toast & marmalade & coffee, I saw who she was, as a little girl, in all the other lives; she was kneeling

under a bush, petting the injured, scabby kitten there, so it wouldn't suffer alone in the weeks before it was crushed under the tires of a car.

In Amsterdam it was raining, in Iowa, the snow had angel-misted over the mangled corn fields where the wild wind howled as it marauded

across the naked burrows & into the open pig barn like a sliced hurt, ripping a black dress apart &, in Paris, a couple softly read the

newspaper & I could see that she was in all *three* places, petting a dying kitten so that she could see it forever—in a perfectly still

mirror—& never take her two eyes off it so she could coax it somewhere, where it could fall out of time & into eternity, just like her. That's what

I saw. When she coaxed me to kiss her & make her real, I saw the ruined kitten, which sits underneath a cold bush inside all love. The sirens

outside were wailing & something was on fire—a long time ago—& we were above it. I can't explain that anymore. But the dead kitten in every

marriage is what we love. It's a coaxing, all this loving, it's a coaxing across a chasm with a kitten in it, way down below us. After that, the

coaxing is mystery, it's a faceless party card. It leads us wherever it needs us. She isn't the hurt kitten. All of that is before us. A long time ago,

before we were true. She is just the imago of the girl petting the injured kitten underneath a bush, so the kitten can fall into eternity & mean

something about love. & happiness is something that gives itself to hurt, so that injured beauty can be real again, & be rescued from history,

which wants to possess it; & to pet an injured kitten during the autumn
when the leaves are a dome & the injured beings squat under them,

waiting on time & whatever else will save them from memory or the
imago of history, so that they're free again to be enveloped by a

lightness that carries them, means we are being kind to history, which
needs us more than we need it; & so the imago of the girl petting the

kitten is art, it is performance for existence, & I can't explain it any
more than that, except to say that coaxing fires something from nothing

into life & I wanted that, anyway. & I wanted a world where a girl was
coaxing an injured kitten to come with her to another place so it wouldn't

be obliterated without one more soft hand caressing it &, besides, to coax
something alive meant that history didn't mean anything greater to me

than what it *could* be, & I wanted that. & I don't know what we thought it
would be: all this entanglement in one another's lives; these mornings

of lovemaking, then silence, those other nights when the fighting
we did, so hard, was like the Meat Cove waves in Nova Scotia that we

stood over on our honeymoon, so shocked to see it: these waves hurling
murderous against the hard-angled defense of rocks . . . & the submitting

beach, receiving all the aftermath—so defenseless, so utterly receptive—
which was history, anyhow—& history's always being submissive to the

facts that create it. History has a dead kitten in it . . . & a set of hands
that miss it all the time as it free-falls. History imitates memory: both are

imaginary friends. Just ghosts. *Maybe history bullies those that ignore it,*
she said. & when she said that, which was after we were fighting, I saw

the girl maybe in Amsterdam or in Paris, or in Iowa or Detroit, petting
the injured cat; she was just kneeling there in the gray dusk, stroking

the kitten's head so it would *know* itself as a body with a hand on its
head, being kind to it, so that the universe could feel what happens

when we act *before* history & give something to it with a kindness
that's before what is true & sad; & it was just beginning to rain, we

could hear its incessant, musical humming on the roof & in the gutters,
on the lawns & in the vulnerable places where birds huddled in nests,

& the raindrops were drenching & drowning the tall trees & also the
Christmas lights so that everything glistened in bright mystery, in beauty,

& history is what we use to fool ourselves that we *aren't* right here,
holding one another & wanting bad for something better; & history's

full of stories & all the unchanged love in all *that.* & all these stories
crush the ignorance of who we once were—if we let them, is what she

said. & maybe the only remedy for an injured history is warm kindness—
that coaxing of something back, from where it retreated from view.

Now she's undoing the buttons on her shirt, she's opening herself up,
so she can see the aging she's worried about; it's winter & the figure

of her body—maybe sunburned by the summer that gave over to autumn
& to winter—that was also the body of the girl in the dream, petting the

injured kitten underneath a bush, is also submissive to the time that's
making it; &, it isn't old or young at all: it's just *figure against a ground*

making it all up. Even this poem's making it all up, so it can coax me to
remember it when I am in an airport hanger, trying to get to Denver. &,

after a while, we train memory to recite life back to us, like it's reciting
a story, a made-up story, a fairytale, a parable with a coma & dead kitten

in it. I didn't make that lie up, History did. & after the sunburn, the red burning, there is a cooling off period that forgives, that releases the

burned skin, the horror. & she drapes the cool bathrobe over her shoulders . . . & she says to me: history never bullies us: all it does is tell

us what to be kind to, when we find it there, shivering like a rain-drenched kitten under a bush. All it does is that. That's it, that's all.

A Stage Play Exposition on Love & Marriage

When the orb arrived, floating to me like a fragment of a petal, a part,
I didn't understand that we fall in love with one part of someone, & not

the whole. & so I cupped the fragment orb in my palm & thought if I
watered it with one-bit sugar & two-bits water, it would come to life.

It didn't. & when the orb turned woman, we were wed, during the hottest
part of summer & the bagpipes, off Broadway, at intermission, welcomed

us to the island so we could lay together, on the open cliffs overlooking
the Atlantic, & practice what love is to the first-night list of sea birds,

flying haphazard over the tortured cliff rocks. & nothing in the first
double-cast of who we were, then & just now, helped us to find anything

out about each other, except that we'd somehow found one another
through a veneration that is a drapery setting composed of blue painted

curtains & a backdrop; & that, to end the stage play, we would have to
dress another stage, over & over, & that would be a blind seat we'd live,

until such time as the dressing rehearsal was over. & she & I were cast
in this stage play so we'd discover that silence is the first act of prayer

that separates the lovers. & that the love song is the overture of spirit,
commanding a presence; & so we would come to life by & though

a series of promenades that joined & separated us, & that is what love is,
the almond orchards said to us—as the ghost-white blossoms fell

to the earth like new, orphaned calves, or like violet wall paper flaking
& falling from the actual walls of Heaven. & to love not just one part

of someone but, instead, to love the whole, one must shuffle through
the blossoms on a night walk, there on the soft earth & gather them all,

all of them in a Juliet hat or in a sombrero & then construct the other,
over & over. & not so that they are whole but, instead, so that the one

putting the white blossoms together, can finally see the full orb,
the beauty first seen, just as it truly was.

Book of Love

"She nods. You were there. And I was there beside you, watching you. On the shore, a long time ago. The wind was blowing, there were white puffy clouds, and it was always summer."

—Hakuri Murakami, *Kafka on the Shore*

Book of Love

An irritated house fly was buzzing itself up & down
the moss green crinkles of a curtain & acting drunk
or high on honey & too much sun. & I'd been studying it,
the fly, because the house was once my house even
though I didn't live there anymore & all my afternoons
& twilight hours were now spent alone, trying to find—
in the pawn shops—a pearl necklace I'd lost somewhere
that had once been strung around a woman's neck
whom I'd never met &, who had but the ghost of
a chance, one day, to meet me for a first date *dance*—
maybe a two-step polka or a streaming little rhumba
at the town's one, wooden-tabled local dance club,
& maybe enjoy a little Sinatra later on—in the wee hours—
spinning alive on the turntable of a room I was renting
in those days when I worked at a job repairing tires
at a tire shop, near the town's library, by that exquisite
little park where the apricot trees grew wild & where
an old watch repairman, drunk on gin, was always
reading a newspaper whose date I could never read,
even with my glasses on. & he would glare at me
when I passed him by. & it was about two hours before
I'd subscribed to the idea that life is independent
of the body & that it is due to the habitation of a spirit
or a rogue ghost in the body that seems to, well, play
an endless game of chalked hopscotch with memory,
or with the physical body, until one or the other of them
grows simply tired & a little bit irritable or hungry,
like a nine-year-old boy who then wanders home
to stretch himself over a bed & sleep till morning,
his hands in back of his head, as if he had all eternity.
& also, crouched there in the sweat of the body,
there's a thief whose whole objective is to abide
in that region of one's spirit until such a time as he,
inside the mystery of time, returns to inhabit a body—
maybe so to become married, or to become involved
in another person's physical realm so as to enter

the soul-bound realm of that other person's body
& then be rehabilitated in it, like he'd been dispatched
to a lover's sanitarium, for to be healed in it.
& maybe I was that man, but I couldn't find
the ghost inside me nor the thief, either. &, besides,
maybe they needed to find *me,* lost in a theater
on the bored side of town where a delicatessen was.
& when neither the thief nor the ghost exists, there's
just the divine & that's what I wanted, anyway.
& I wanted it with a woman I hadn't met yet.
&, on the morning of the day I'd find the woman
who'd worn the pearl necklace—& find her
roaming through the fragrant almond groves
no less, inside an oval peep hole that I paid cash
to gaze into, at a peep show that had opened up,
ignobly, inside an old, closed burlesque theater
near a delicatessen where they still served donuts,
I saw a policeman pull up in his squad car & park it,
silently, behind a gas station. & he sat a moment
& pulled his sunglasses over his pig-face, so he
could settle himself in some kind of conviction
he'd been planning. & I watched him push the car
door open & then close & lock it & start walking.
& the policeman, strolling the sidewalks alone
on his afternoon beat, ran his billy-club across
the white picket fences of the gentle side streets
of the neighborhood as he looked for a woman
whom he'd met on a traffic stop (who'd been
crying after a quarrel with her husband, and after
she'd been drinking at a dive bar they called Davy's
Sow) &, all he could do, as he lit up cigarette after
cigarette on his mid-morning walk through the
neighborhood, was remember that when he'd pulled
her over, her, in her Vienna Blue 54' Studebaker
Commander & then, had asked her to step out
of the car & pace-walk herself in a straight sober
line down the yellow highway strip of the road

where the oncoming cars could pass one another
like stars, she did so as he'd instructed—& she
stepped lightly, like a simple working girl just off
shift at the corner life insurance agency, in her
lime green work dress & her pointed-toe pumps.
& she lifted the soft air with her two right fingers
while walking steadily down the yellow line
while holding something practical & invisible—
like a dog's leash—in her left hand, which fell
lower still, so she looked exactly like she was
walking a black poodle over a circus wire, or
perhaps stepping reverently & about to curtsey
before a king or a queen. & once, a book fell open
so that it spilled all the hidden cards out of it
that had been wedged in the dried pages for years
upon years, like old lover's secrets, & the cards—
those that had been stored in the book of love—
simple kings, jokers, red 10s & queens—lay there,
spilled across the street for anyone's taking,
& they were so inviting & inscrutable that even
the illiterate street sweepers could scoop them up,
pocket them in shirts or place them, like surprises,
in the elbowed crooks of the town's planted trees
for anyone looking for a card game to join, or play,
or maybe even for a ghost & a thief to marvel at—
& then, by circumstance or by embodiment, *take*.
& then pocket for themselves for next evening's
harvest dance at the school gymnasium, or for
the goodluck's close, near the town's exit gate.
& the policeman remembered it, the way she
looked up at him, trusting *him* with her most
shameful, if drunken hour. & so he'd decided,
irrationally, to walk up to her house, right up
the steps to check on her & maybe make her
walk another straight line down the house steps
to meet him at the opened gate of her house,
near the sidewalk &, if her husband, a plumber

named Darren was there, they'd shake hands
& look each other over before the policeman
took his wife away, on new charges. & the book
never changes, only the cards in it shift themselves
like hands roaming dryly—knuckle over knuckle—
in a ceaseless game of shuffle. & the thief & ghost
never change either, except for their places,
which is why the game is always so irrational,
& so very interesting, if divine, all the same.

Jeqon, The Inciter Angel (Echo Park)

In Echo Park, in LA,

some time ago when I was lost in thought,
        and feeding the small, irritated birds

that sorted and darted there to the lake, to land in it like soft,
        feathered dragon lizards or angels—

those demented ones who have been tempted by carnal desires,
        by loose relations, drugs, cash,

and even by the needle's soft injectable radiance like these lost junkies,
condemned to wander because they were led astray

        by Jeqon, the Inciter Angel—

I found myself provoked by the one still thought
        that
        after I'd wandered Venice Beach
        and then drove south

to Redondo Beach to watch the slow escalation of waves
plundering the beach in a fever, in a slow, solipsistic

redundancy like a record playing, that I had become
        hopelessly caught,

and trapped in the Beach Boy's song,
        Don't Worry Baby.

Jeqon strolls up to me intimately.
        His wide face,

like a mixture of tea leaves and salt, even kelp.

>   Tells me

he arrives this way, to match place. Tells me
I became enraptured in the song after drinking alone
>   in a dive bar in Santa Monica,

while the song played on the juke box.

>   I recall
the woman who pressed it
>   to play.

That she was one of those tired women
who play with fantasy,

with the illusion of their facial settings, their lips,
their sores for eyes, their languid hair,

and that the fellow she was with
>   —a motorcycle dude—

wrapped his arms around her thin, desolate frame and through his liquor,
>   mouthed the lyrics,
"don't worry baby, everything will turn out alright . . ."

>   ~

Jeqon tells me
>   one becomes lost

>   in such a song
because the hero of tragedy must always be strong,
>   you know, like a vast consequence

of himself.

Do you feel that, he asks me—this vast consequence of yourself—
this excited facade in masquerade form? Look at the man there:

The man in the bar there, the one whose vagrancy
is lost in her

and look at how he is
building it up inside himself for so long, like he's
an engine—just a combustible opportunism

trying to drag race against the action and time in order
to heighten it:

well, that's the consequence of weakness
inside untrue arguments.

And then me—

I am asking Jeqon what I have to do with this
and he wakes me up,

underneath the ficus trees in Echo Park,

just as a man on a stingray rides past us,
his stinking body the aroma of perished days gone by,

and I am awakened inside the song.

Hear it inside the lovely lotus beds, there in the lake.
The lyric,

I can't back down

because I've pushed the other guys too far,

and then that she makes me come alive,
and makes me wanna to drive when she says,

don't worry baby, everything will turn out alright.

Jeqon tells me,

*you are entranced by the guitar solo,
bounding behind the chorus refrain—*

and you fell this way, years ago, in a car with a blond girl

who took you from the temporal order, mesmerized you.

This articulation of your entrapment can be traced back then—
       in your young manhood—

when you were vulnerable to the *enchantment*
of touch and aroma.

Tells me, you are incoherent, especially after sex.

And that all love and romance are cut in a flavor,
       a nostalgia, like this song,

and so it is that you are under the illusion that nothing
can go wrong with you.

And that is how you revolve, like a 45 record, around
       this loquacious assimilation
       of what you think's divine.

Now, we are walking up through Echo Park.

Now—alongside a small bar whose patrons are born
       in heroin addiction, tattoos, and elegance—

he shows me how it is the slight woman there,
the one whose face resembles a carp face
       with reddened lips

and the morning star rising up in her lit eyes,
       is
the agony and the ecstasy for you;

      she is the one
whom the sons of God make their beds with,
      he tells me,

and it is for that reason—you with her now—

that you will enter that song again,
      the Beach Boy's song,

and through your entrapment there, your maya,
      your involution of power,

and through your reconciliation with all this
famished music

and all this deep impermanence and emptiness,
      you will save face.

Monique Jean

Youthful beauty & introverted solitude spoke together,
& neither one of them could manage to give up
the bathroom vanity, for fear of either leaving
the safe room, & so a marriage was out of the question,
& the result was dogs. Not humans. Just dogs.
& when she stands, now, in the mirror, mixing
the soap to cleanse her fragile, magazine face,
the dogs, like large brown leaves, lounge at her feet,
& I think it makes her feel safe, or fresh. Complete.
& the frenetic, subtropical bugs in the palm trees
argue in the isle of lanterns &, on the isle of dogs,
she'll graduate this life when she lets go of the leash.
& as she strolls—like a crooked, half-asleep avocet
across the gulf beach & through the sea oats & the yaupon—
I remember that, when I first saw her, asleep as she hid
behind her sister, that she jumped free, up onto
the shoulders of a triangle of cheerleaders & it
was amazing, how she could do that, half-asleep.
& be like a star that, blazing awake, is wondrous. & I believe
that I fell in love with her then, like a lost dog.
Surrounding the isle of dogs & the islands of the blessed,
a few 70s cars laid around—shiny, confident, explicit—
& surrounding the high school, the football players ran.
& surrounding the football field, on the track,
the cheerleaders jumped & clapped & chanted
for the practicing frat house of football players
who were running protest laps around the track
because one of them had smoked weed the night
before & someone—the whole team—had to pay,
& the isle of mist was nothing, just old smog,
& I was hiding in there, but I'll get to me later.
& the lethargic, wise fool of sleep was waking me.
& doddling there, half-asleep in the leafy shade
of the autumnal, sick, decaying sycamore trees,
the double-walkers, the exact orphic look-alikes
of everyone of us, squatted by an old can fire—

it'd been lit to flame by a few haunted men who'd
once been one of the invisibles, those who hide
& are hidden, but these folks had been kicked out
of the whole group for not appearing in public
to get the usual cash handouts on the side beams
of highways, where the itching eye of rag doll girls
sold roses—& I was one of the invisibles, I was. & I was
staying hidden behind a clever scarf & a hat & I was
mimicking a high school cross-country runner—a kid—
& I'd been crossed through skin & bone by a double,
&, through the haggard, berserk sycamore trees, I could
see her, a blond girl whose face tried to escape & hide
& maybe even disguise itself in a bonnet of bloomed hair
surrounding it—her face—& she was unconscious
& just going through the motions in her little red skirt
& her cream white cheerleader sweater, & half-asleep,
& she was waiting to be doubled, so she could meet me.
&, later, after the midsummer's madness turned russet
with autumn & we'd fallen in love together, we met
at a carnival—this was after Halloween—& we saw
the clowns & the iron lady with the mustache & the
jugglers all gambling, throwing cards & dice in a game,
& we snuck past them, holding hands as we crept
through the pick-up lot of circus equipment trucks
& the footprint-moulage of shattered scotch bottles
&, pausing together, under an ash tree, we kissed,
& I couldn't be invisible anymore, nor could she.

Lucille Marie Jean

Lucille was in a stage play about an illicit affair between an actress
& a postman when I first set eyes on her. We met at a donut shop

when I stumbled in for a cup of coffee. She was working the counter.
This was in a small theater district in Pittsburg, maybe in Hamtramck,

& maybe the play was set in the furtive 40s or maybe in the decadent,
pompous 80s, it was hard to tell because of the last second call

for performers to take their acting positions before the curtains rose.
After that happened, all the actors rushed into place & it was chaos.

A prompt box at the center of the stage organized everyone, even me.
When the lights panned left to right across the stage, I saw her

in her first play to the balcony. & she was Italian, a brunette in a short
Euro haircut & dressed in a cropped top & a jean jacket, with opaque

jewelry spilling like a street corner fortune around her neck. The wealth!
She wore a crinoline dress that shimmered with the air & horseshoe stars,

& she wore white pumps so that when she walked, or strutted to
meet the hapless postman, me, the air behind her was a comet. Now, I

was stoned in love with the way she smoked cigarettes & set her mouth
in a style of downstage lipstick that resembled a theater party. & she

wore a grin in her smile that mostly kept a secret. So much of the play
had nothing to do with love or desire. Mostly, it involved eidetic memory

& learning how to sing softly in the dark or have sex without formalizing
all the details. & when I fell in love with her, it was at the back door,

after the play had ended & the houselights had softened on us,
which was just the high moon. On that night, she wore a brown coat

& she kissed me at a punk rock show to the song, "The Tide is High,"
& the beam projector shined its optical mixing of yearning, all over us.

Punk

In the University district / a bird / in a fur coat
smoked alive a thin cigarillo

and the band inside the bar / blasted a melody apart.
What part of the Universe is opened alive / by punk guitars?

Limitation disappears on dope / in music / in love
the Angel at the Dystopian gate / whispered to me . . .

You are a bursting boundary / and the kiss
on the lips / eternalizes you / the angel of Six-String said.

I was young / I didn't understand that all human light
is Catharsis / is stumbling awake / at dawn / so in love /

the moon spread all over your fingers / the stars
dripping from coat sleeves / washed in light / in vapor / and baptized

in a cave of phantoms / and that's how
we arrive in love / I said to the woman / in a fur coat / and

isn't it surrender? / Isn't that the form love takes / to costume us?
It's alright the angel murmured / we blow up /

we masquerade / we undress. / Punk / is the form the Trickster Angel
always takes to flip our consciousness / into a bonfire / into a brave face.

I think I will kiss you until you are a ringing guitar, / said
the woman in an animal coat the color of straw.

Her eyes / apocalyptic / naked. / Her face like the soft glass
of a rising moon.

After the kiss / a neon light across the bar's marquee flickered.
Love is a naked payment / a ransom for defense / for fear / for yearning.

We only awaken when the rhythm guitar and the vocalist ignite the stars /
and the drummer's cymbals / —a mercenary soldier's— / crash.

We knelt down across the street / holding hands in the salted moonlight
while two women shot dope. Old cars / parked there / like castles.

Praying / is conflagration / the one woman said to us.
While her sister tied her arm off / then shot up.

The bird woman in a fur coat / kissed me awake / again and again
so that I could be a spinning jenny / a spirit-writing.

I was pilgrim then / not yet at zenith / so young.
We are baptized / the angel said / in breath / in light / in awe / in glory.

Contemplation on Covetousness & Love

Sometimes, walking alone, I see where the wind goes.
Nothing moves in a straight line. Only our lies, & even that

is a lie. & once, a long time ago, when I was trying out
for the circus, I dated the woman who swallowed knives

just to prove she was dangerous & stronger than her uncle
& his bar room brawl friends. & we'd hang out, behind

the trailer where her costumes—bright-green bubble dresses,
wedge & slip dresses & sequin dresses . . . & pillbox hats,

berets, cartwheels—lay spilled all over a table & we'd
sip scotch & talk about Spanish poetry & the Ramones,

& we'd walk along a stream, holding hands, & that's where
I first saw where the wind goes. & across a heath, where

even the grass seemed purple, we saw how covetousness
glistens as it clings to small plants &, in the shelterbelt,

where the trees formed a kind of wall, we watched her
life go up in blaze & flame, like a vulnerable conifer on fire

& that's because the wind-stream of life—& how it's actually
imparted—is infectious . . . & can I confess that I chased her?

her pine needles up in flame, on fire—& with a mug of water—
just to put her out? & shortly thereafter, I bought a small hut

& we lived quietly there together, but she suffered in an
hysterical state where she felt she'd lost both her hands,

& love is so inestimable . . . & it's like a form of wealth & so
I'd kiss the ghost spaces there, in her absent hands, *because.*

& I'd sing to her at night a small, favorite French pathetique,
& garble the words just enough so she'd feel memorialized,

& loving-kindness is vivid prana, & it's a type of song, & it
is so brief, this life, like brandy: everything we do, is true.

The Angel of Yearning Speaks to Me

                1.

On the boat, yes, there it is. You see it like a wisp of memory
drifting off the gallery of a cottonwood tree branch.

We were on Michael's boat. So full of yearning, we
dove into the black, disheartened lake water,

just teenaged boys trying to discover the door of what
every deeper revealing place conceals.

Dove far down to grab the mysterious weeds
growing upwards from sand.

Felt the weird weeds grab us like drunk, desperate girls.
Michael toked on a joint. Said he liked it.

Paul was so high we thought he'd get his ankles
tangled in the rough, ragged brown anchor rope,

we thought he'd cut himself, trip, and cut his head open.
So we pulled him off it and he wrestled us.

We hurled him over the side,
into the demented, pickle-black water.

It must have been July. Someone's barbecue lit.

Badfinger, *Day After Day, Baby Blue,* blasting out.
Pete Ham hung himself, is what you dreamed

late at night, his lifeless body dangling there
like a torpid side of strung fish. I bled Pete Ham.

We caught fish. Cut them to bits. We were so high
we forgot about them. Flies crawling all over

their uninhabited, erupted, bloated bodies.
Do their souls—defunct, departed alms—lift up
and fly away, like unashamed girls kissing

each other with no faces? No faint murmurs?
After we boys, drunk, kissed the up-north girls

visiting from a beach town I've long forgotten,
we smoked more weed, we drank beer,

and I approached the redheaded girl that

nobody else wanted. She cried so hard against me,
her night mouth smelling like potato chips,

cigarettes and beer; and, to comfort her,
I softly kissed her and she pushed her body

hard against mine and she whispered to me,
"nobody knows my secret hiding place."

The trees above the lake caught wide breezes.
One of them caught an *ikiryo* ghost

(she was telling me about Japanese ghosts
as we kissed to the protest of frogs)

and the redhead cried super hard—
just like a multi-cell cluster thunderstorm.

Years later, Paul—bearded, drunk on tequila—
told me

she'd died in a car crash outside

of Oscoda. God, the yearning in

every car crash, whispers the angel
of demarcation, to me.

2.

Nobody knows my hiding place

is what we whisper to one another

when we are wearing desire

like an incarnation in a costume.

All we are is a definite sense

and a masquerade. And that's just time.

Yearning is time's essential paramour.

3.

Those nights, in the University District, we'd
smoke opium, let moonlight fume our eyes.

After gigs the bands would stand together,
smoking, drinking, fucking off, nothing to hide.

(Except for his small shipwrecked tiger hands
punching a homosexual outside the bar,

all I can see is the band's roadies, breaking down.
The bouncer, his pug hands, punching a boy.

To deny the yearning, he'd just wait, hit again.
I finally threw a bottle; the band drove off.)

Oh, I remember the Italian girl's red pepper lips
and that while we were kissing—super drunk

on vodka—that she pushed hard against me—

vibrating in a faint, black intoxicated glow—

and we lay there together, against a car's

cool front hood like we were spiritually welded.

Not love, not desire, not lust . . . just *yearning,*

yes yearning is what kindles us at the margins,

and we chase it, oh yes we chase it, we do—

and I swear to God this is true—we chase it

to stop being *provoked.* We chase it to be
the water again. Water, embracing life again.

Yearning provides what impulse divines in us.

"It is ok—"

the Italian girl whispered to me afterwards, afterwards

in that bed where we very tenderly, very forcefully

went way too far. "Does going too far condemn us?"

she asked. "Are we damned by what we
won't admit to ourselves? Does going too far

wither us like dry lilac or does it marry us in fragrance?"

Is any of this even true? Do I smell her soft breath now?

Over her lip, a lovely round mole like a seed.
Her autograph eyes blinking something I

couldn't quite ever read. "We go too far with each

other to make life last," she said
to the empty afternoon. "We love each other

by breaking all our taboos. Isn't that right?"
Our bodies: Blinking lights. Testing grounds.

Echoes that only God creates for us to sing.
Just diamonds against dark black time.

Is it any surprise we call each other
sweetheart?

"We went too far and I liked it," she said.

                4.

"*Went way too far* is the providence yearning—"
says the angel of nobody knows my dwelling place.

"Yearning is what all dwelling's made of—
before every aroma of your seed pod bursts.

One consecrates the body inside stirred yearning.
One temples every kiss, every hot body's twist."

I said: "Oh Love Angel of the aftermath of sex—
of physical fights, of swimming, of kissing,

of drowning way too high on opium and blues—
am I the bog, the pond, the greedy hands?

We are the body that goes way too far.
We are the body that burns its taboos alive.

We go too far because we are going, going
we are gone. We wear these cloudy shoes.

We walk these cloudy shoes right down into
tomorrow's untitled ground. Isn't that enough?"

And the angel said to me—his orchestral wings
beating back and forth like red oriental fans

swishing small moonbeams up above him
so that the air was speckled in moons, in stars—

"nothing is alive in this life until we *effuse* it.
Our memories, like aromatic tea. Like spice.

We must go too far. Only then do we testify
to the senses." "To be grabbed in your eyes is to lose
the fear of my body," the Italian woman said

to me, didn't she? "So pin me, tantalize me,
play me for keeps; there is no end," she said.

        5.

Years later, behind a bleak, desolate building
in a northern town, I wished all the yearning

away. It's too heavy, I said.
The drizzled broken memory angels

crouched on the wooden crates; they were cutting fruit . . .

Three, four, five of them silently laughing at me.

One beside himself, staring intently at me.
Hostile, jealous, humid, his hands like kale.

6.

Years later, in a rental place high up

on a rugged southern river bluff
my wife let me take her naked photograph,

one, two, three, four times.
Outside the closed bedroom door,
shuffling down the wooden hallways,

the angels of broken memory clanged on,
restless, listening for what we were up to.

"To have my body," she whispered to me, "you'll
have to drop that camera and you'll have to

abandon your own body,
and you'll have to let go of some secret dwelling place

deep inside of you—
and then you must let me have it, own it,

let me play it for keeps,"
she whispered, grinning like a planet's outer ring

and, oscillating between kissing me and pushing
herself away from me, here, on an unmade bed

so that she could get herself up,

smell the smoked auroras
of the pagan night and listen to the mockingbirds

imitating the forlorn sing-along
of the Mississippi River, at Natchez,

my wife, satisfied, turned back to me, grinned, said,

". . . and go too far with me, push yourself
into the vagrant, nomadic shape

of a wild storm inside the book of love

and get on with it," and so I did.

In the Almond Groves

"Madonna, mistress, I would build for thee
an altar deep in the sad soul of me;
and in the darkest corner of my heart,
from mortal hopes and mocking eyes apart,
carve of enameled blue and gold a shrine
for thee to stand erect in, image divine."

—Charles Baudelaire, *To a Madonna*

Confession

Every night the same glow. Some life trying to get in.

I used to think it was my father, long gone
come to visit with me as a grizzled old vagrant.
His suit, his hat, his empty, penetrating eyes gazing across at me.

Do I believe it is my father?

My confessions to him process nothing
of who he *was* to me.
Only this inner counting as I wait for his return . . .
Do I think it is my mother, trying to hold me as I cry?

Maybe it is my distant lover from some long time ago.

Maybe that's all that memory truly is—
just sensory images and an inner counting
until we . . . what? master waiting? Our steps,

part of an older saunter?
Well, I waited on a visitation by weird *others* to claim me.

Struck by visions, I crept out there to meet them in the dark.

I waited for hours on a prayer rug. Knees crossed.
Oil, incense, a prayer wheel. An owl hooting above.

I woke to a white paper moon. Bright stars.

What is it about sleeping, forgetting, remembering?
Is it the clairvoyant imagination, so fired?
Is loneliness just a sleeping, a forgetting, a remembering?

That I could suspend time for myself?
Enter the absolute emanations of Spirit?

In the tangled shrubs, hesitant beings. I *saw* them.
Shrouded, hooded, like trumpet vines.

My father's Imago whispers to me,
you are the ineffable magnitude.
When the hands that seek you, take you,

you are just atoms-to-atoms, strip-searched for meaning.

You are the love-light divine.
The observatory. The beacon. *Free.* You will find what light calls to you.

And then a *nectarivorous angel,* a pollen bat,
vibrates over me: It says:

Maybe love is the one applied masquerade we spirit dance to.

To uplift us in prayer. Maybe a light in another calls us to love it.

Maybe supplication is how we begin to appraise all our losses.

How we curate life's aesthetic paradoxes. Its lies, Its truths.

The white almond tree blossoms in the San Joaquin Valley

falling to the ground so erotic, so fragrant, so spent, just as the others

come alive with naked bridal aroma, resembling—to me—

both a nuptial and *a funeral . . . What we seek to keep, we lose;*

what we lose returns to us by the hand fulfilling all its absence;

we are lost and found again in the time that renders us in twilight . . .

and we are rendered in memory and loss, in a sleeping beauty awakening

there in the almond orchards; our body, flung out in aromatic petals; . . .

we're made of spirit-shattered light. A beauty impossible to define.

For a long while I sat there, amazed by stars. By a grief
so very secret I could never tell it.

By a confession in a voice adrift,
far, far away from me. By an accuracy that cannot be read.

Confession is an act of spirit; it proves that the body
is an historical fact, and yet completely ahistorical. A hotel space.

Something hiding in the fruit tree said it.
It was bodiless, nothing of it; a spirit flare
in which the whole world appears, that's it, that's all.

And the name is just a feathered bird seeking refuge
in the crow's nest of another's boat—in some other life—
rocking there on the choppy seas.

And what we remember is just the form of the dream
and not the dream itself, which comes true later.

And even then, the gazer liberates into empty being.

I don't carry roses to fool myself on any summer evening now.

Nor do the florid stars
rising over the city park's shell-work

of standstill shards—its glassware, so star-lit—

remember any part of my name.
Except how it is I pray.

Love

Something was playing with me in the almond orchards, it
        wasn't her,

                    &

it was leaping just like a small black bird through
        the white petals, but it wasn't a bird either, but maybe an angel
being,

                    &

it was showing me that love is play—& that it is as soft as two
small feet that don't touch anything at all when they land,

except maybe the light most glad of all, which is
        delight,

which is love's business, the bird said. & then I saw it
        thud on a collapsed apparel of white blossoms

so that
they were suddenly bruised, turned yellow, even rotting,

                    &

love is the light most glad of all that receives the wound & gives
new life & light to it too,
the bird said to me, so it can be healed & so that it can be delighted.

& it—the angel being—picked up the wounded, yellowed, injured petal
in its beak & then it flew away with the petal, through the infernal sky

& through the corridor of all the mirrors, until all I could see
        was where everything physical fails, is completely lost

in sunlight, in the tormented of array of bleached clouds,
        which is memory, forgetting itself & dropping into the coma.

& sacred memory is what awakens in the petals,
in one another too, whenever we give life to love.

Wound Healing

"for it was their injured love that made them do it"
—Milan Kundera

When I cried, I was crying for all of my lifetimes,
& something inside of her knew it. Like maybe
she was remembering me when I was a potato farmer,
in Ireland, & she was holding me after I'd cut my
finger off with an axe, or a wood saw or hoe, & so
she held me tightly as I heaved out my sorrow,
my ache & all my woes. & you know, the stream
of our livingness is a white beam with poppies,
like florid memories, on it. & so she knew I'd been
quite violent, at one point in my journey & even
not quite civil, in *this* lifetime with her. & she could
seemingly see just how the sin of something floats,
then embeds in the tactile nature of our skin so
we can feel it flaring in us as we reenact it alive
with another. & so she held me then, harder, &
leaned into my face & told me I *wasn't* him, not
anymore. & that the old Irish hospital I was in,
all those slipstreams ago, was stone rubble now,
like a collapsed bone skeleton in some green field.
& that the stream of light moving through me,
just now, with her, was inseparable from how we
reconfigure in a body, in a chateau, or in a hotel,
just to awaken again as a new resident, healed alive.
& with somebody we've known all along, down
the slipstream of time. & something in me, then,
saw in her face that she was a Scottish field nurse,
at bedside with me. & she was holding out this
hidden washcloth of opposites—of the wounded
& the healed one together—in one form. & so
she pulled one of the poppies off of it, for it was
part narcotic so that it could heal me—so I'd be
more patient & pastoral within it, here in my body,
& she spread the wound all over me, like medicine,
like she was cleansing me with just my own pain.
& washing my body with what comes, just after.
& she pointed, softly, through the window where

together we could see a soft bed of white flower
petals, almond petals. & it felt like the old hospital
bed I'd laid in but, at the same time, it was now.
& I was with the woman who was now my wife.
& the wound of all my lifetimes, that violence,
that resistance to a light most glad of all that
heals & transforms what was pain into deep love,
gave over to an overcoming of that world. & into
a healing into *this* world, right here & now.

Delight

"One semblance circles me, a single movement"
—Pablo Neruda

We're at it again, in the bed, on the bed, all over the bed,
rambling & rolling around in the almond orchards

where we first met & embraced one another like fireworks,
like the glowing thief & ghost of something trying to leave

the prison of separation & loneliness just to be paroled,
like scheduled, aromatic scents into the final divine,

& when I touch her in that place where the soul could be saved
from being in just one identity, she throws her head backwards,

her face then, truer than mere appearance & ghost-white now
& then suddenly reddened, & overwhelmed in pleasure

& quickly at the abolition of all boundary &, in response, I roll
my eyes upward, trying again to see where it is she's rising to,

where it is she goes to, when that impediment wall, that skin,
is breached into heaven's language, into spirit into substance

& back &, for a moment, I can't contain what's uprising
into me—me, still on top of her—for it's like a ghost-scatter,

thick with a spray of white almond petals exploding themselves
upward, into my whole person. & I'm the thief & so I lapse

into intoxication, into that lawless, riotous, disobedient force
that finds its namelessness in me, in us, & she laughs then, at me,

at the criminal in me that's lost & concluding itself in her,
& she wiggles my face back down, in to her, so she can kiss

the affluence from my face & make it hers, ours, forever,
& be a part of the divine that will remember the delight, after

we're long gone & roaming through the almond groves—
in search of where the beginning of delight was, or is, again.

In the Almond Groves, Highway 5, San Joaquin Valley

"It cost me labor and love to see what you see"
—Miguel Hernandez

I reach up and I shatter a storm of white almond blossoms
    all over my head, my shoulders and across the dirt
with my hands as I extend, as I blend my fingers
    into the baptismal lightning of the fragrant white flowers.

When we touch a thing possible, we can no longer dread
    a nothingness—for it is alive.

The angel of the orchards whispered this to me as the hard traffic,
    scorching Highway 5 in the San Joaquin Valley, bullied forward
off ramp into the dried towns of Bakersfield, Fresno, Barstow, Clovis,
    and the singing angel, a small ricochet of lemon light,
said again to me: the soul, an attendant to consciousness,
    listens to the absences, to the nothingness and lo—
we are able to represent ourselves in the body
    of another person; this is the lover's way; like honey
from another hive, unseen for years. It hides, the angel
    whispered to me, underneath the shadows, in the melodies;
and it hides inside our eyes; and it lives in the eyelashes.

    To *Love*, the angel said to me, is to begin to speak
with the babble-tongue of the magpie, which is naked, alive.
And then we can chant the Quintessence of Spirit, of Love.
You will come to sing the knowing of your lover's song.

In the almond orchards, trespassing through the bridal veils and up
    through the wedding garlands of the angelic white blossoms
the yellow-billed magpie arrives; it's an extravagance of black, blue,
    white, and a painter's smear of a green tail.

The yellow-billed magpie has flown here from the oak woodland's edge.
    He is you—back from your past, the angel demurred to me . . .
listen to the harsh audible calls that resemble a curious scratching
    at someone's wooden doorway; listen to the incessant,

peppered hopscotch of its pinched babbling. It is you, *the angel
told me; and the fragrant blossoms are* her, *at your wedding,
and vice versa: . . . it's both. You are both unbodied & yet,* solid.
*Together you must change shapes in order to find one another;
your souls will wander: gathering to them these blossoms
for the void in you that you long to jubilate—with all this
glad noise, with all this devotion; and that is the pardon
of death, the angel said:* this *love. Love is the unchanging
breath in the body that we borrow, that we inhabit—alas—
for just a spell of time, until the season ripens the berries . . .
and the curious rats there, underneath, sniff & nibble . . .
while the lovers go on with their exultant singing . . .
and in the end, in the void, all that's left is the singing . . .*

My wife was waving to me from the car, a quick hello.
You see, we were driving to Big Sur. This was when we
fell in love again with the fertile odors of the hot air,
the immortal perfume that was a weeping into delirium—
in those almond groves where the jubilee of love is . . .
and where the exultant, jubilant, magnetic singing is—
and with one heart we could beat from, till the end.

Love's Body

   &

&

because she was intelligent—she was grown up now, a wife & a lover of many years & she wasn't at all fooled by me anymore—

by my temptation to hide from her, to vanish into a dream—

she pushed her orchid-white hands down hard on my chest, the wedding ring glistening on her left finger, her eyes like a raven's,

& then she fixed me there on the bed & she pinned me there

&

she kissed me super-charged on the lips so I could feel her bones,

&

she whispered that old age is a running brook that comes from the breath, like a tangle of birds released from a sentence

&

it's so quickly done, my pilgrim that runs so drunkenly into the sun.
& she looked me hard in my pupils / until we held it there / one.

Quick Postcard
(The Angel of the Ravel District, Barcelona)

At the Hostel de los Ramos, on the balcony
looking down at us, a group of couples
jumped & jived to dance club mix. To techno.

A woman in a silver skirt waved seductively at me,
to everyone strolling down the street, & her lover
—black-crow hair, a jaw like a hammer—

bullied her with Spaniard machismo & after-dinner kisses
& just far enough away from the balcony
so that we couldn't see what other excitements happened
between them. The air sparkled.

Barcelona's crazy; it's an enlargement of desire; it never stops,
my wife exclaimed to me as we hiked up the avenue
in & then and out of the Ravel district
where two lovers held tight to one another
& kissed beneath a sagging Sycamore tree.
The woman let him sip her beer.

I think we love an emptiness in us until it enlarges—
& then we make a world in *that,* I said.

My wife scooped me closer to herself & patrons
—across the street from us—watched soccer
at an outside bar where beer & tapas were served.

The air, salty now. Parakeets singing in palm trees,
just out of the ear's range. The taste of the evening
somehow numbing our tongues with garlic,
with hot peppers . . .

& a raven-haired woman
hand-to-hand dancing with an old man
who had been playing a fiddle underneath

the cathedral's gothic glow . . . the light of it youthful,
beautiful, fermenting . . .

"& the pirate life of the heart is always
an immigrant within a desire,"
the angel of the Ravel district offered,
hearing us speaking to one another.

"*It's a thief's journal with an ache,*" he whispered—
"*& it's a desire that forever tries to save its own life
in the impassioned arms of another;*

&—you know—
it awakens in love's election,"
the angel said to us there . . .

"& to be constantly present to one another
is the gift of stepping into a true revolt,
for the consent to breach the distance—
& I mean the distance
where beauty and reality are identical,
& that's a love, without any fear,"

the angel said to us as we ran together
across the Las Ramblas into the old city.

*

& this is the part the angel told me to remember:

mendicants & revelers singing
Spanish military anthems & other travelers—
just sweet-hearted people dancing together
until even their histories
didn't matter anymore;—

& the night heat changeless, like mezcal,
& the soft albino light of the street lamps

just like white fermented beans
glowing moodily
under the night's
cabbage colors,
its rainbow sparkles . . .

You see, this is what we *both* remember,
& what I'm writing to you now:

Love & Beauty are a testimony of Spirit that grace granted
into the incarnated vision of this world,

*& to give it away—so that it nourishes others
into delight
is all the night parade asks us to do . . .*

& but for each other, & for the sake of the song,
we could knock the lamp shade from the moon
so its blessed light spills all over us

just to give it all up / just to hold the beloved

&

to touch the beautiful in us that can never change.

Sunday Morning Prayer

If time is eternal in Heaven, I'd rather be temporary
& in your arms

as the fire burns in the fireplace & the ice-rain falls
steadily outside

covering the entire avenue in ice-white pebbles.
& if love

is a measurement of how we've surrendered to mystery,
how we've become vapor somehow

inside all the love songs on the radio's static ethers,
I'd rather

be a ruddy fisherman in a bog—still alive—slogging through it
for another fresh pearl

so that I can again offer it to you.
& if spirit is an almond orchard where the flower blossoms

are the dropped white lace
of the seven angels of the apocalypse

abandoning all their their maps for the route to love,
I'd rather be lost in all that, than to be at another church,

hearing again why it is we've sinned
by laying down together

on a bed of white almond blossoms before marriage.
& if rapture is just spirit

stretching itself in a yoga ritual so as to feel itself alive
in a physical body,

Oh I'd rather lay here in it—enjoying it—
thanking the sweet aromatic air

for all my faithful fingers holding precisely & tightly
all your writhing incredible bodily life

inside them, so as to never feel you out of home.
& if you are all I have to love today,

you, double flame
of consent, you, floral life of delight,

you, woman of the almond groves
whom I've found I can never leave

and who still fits around one ice cream-white finger
a simple wedding ring

as you stroll, singing a path of sweetness
throughout all the rooms,

then I'll take *that* roadway you offer,
to all that is God.

Contemplation in a Small City Park
w/ Apricot Trees

I've been sitting alone again, on this green park bench under the shade
trees in that forgettable city park where I used to feed the comatose,

easy going pigeons with my scraps of listless day-old bread,

& I've been reflecting on the time that's gone by, especially through
my stopwatch, & I've been listening with my whole entire heart

to Skeeter Davis's "The End of the World" & "I Can't Believe It's Over,"
& maybe it's the season, what with all these summer breezes blowing

immoral & transgressive through the simple apricot trees & maybe, also,
the way the pigeons seem to ignore it, in their easy, deliberate lassitude

&, when I feed them, I can fall asleep again into that remembering
that will always ignore the present. & maybe I'll remember all the old
        rooms

& the soft bottles of wine we consumed, while listening to "Moondance"
on that old, lawless turntable & how, one night, I cooked her dinner

by candlelight, & we drew ourselves a warm bath & we snuggled into it.
& maybe time's contemplation is like a cooing dove, eager for bread,

& so we allow it & we follow it, dumbed by its lasting, immutable
phonetics &, like two beings sitting still on a bench, one talks
        & one listens.

        *

& I've been in that commandment of love, that contemplation again
where the Dharma edict calls up memory & recall, & so time is

Dionysian & full of reverie & rapture & it's also unhinged & seditious,
& thick with old smells & all those sad morphine fragrances

that the self—by its own to surrendering into a submissive willingness—
can become lost & oddly captive in, like a blindfolded prisoner

in a rowboat. & maybe, sitting here on this lonesome park bench
with my little transistor radio on & dialing down the long band

I hear, in the static AM radio fuzz, The Glaser Brothers, that country
music trio from Spaulding, Nebraska,
        crooning
"Ain't It All Worth Living," & "Through the Eyes of Love."

&, maybe, just because of all this, I'm no longer in control of myself
& I'm just slip-sliding, like a ready-made drunk quickly lit on lime juice

& gin, & I'm all alone & I'm readying myself to say my evening prayers,
under the first carnival stars.

& maybe *all* contemplation arrives through music's deep refractory haze,
its soft Decalogue of romance & remembering,

& maybe I'll hear the multitude of all those finite years just now

as the sumptuous young mother rolls the child by me in a baby stroller
&, behind her, the little dog follows after them on a leash
        & the father, so young

in his soft red beard, follows still behind, chatting on his cell phone.

& maybe all life can be seen through the eyes of love, & that's why
it's all so worth living.

& once, in a room dim with dusk-light, I sat so still on a couch
I could feel the streams of red blood moving in me, like laudatory

commandments through my ears,
& I knew I was waiting for something or for someone,

but I couldn't see just who,
& sometime later, after all the sirens of the evening's torment lessoned,

I saw in the bathroom mirror someone else's face, someone not me
who would become something in me

&, later—relaxed & stretched out & drinking a beer, my legs
dangling over the other end of the couch—

I turned the transistor radio volume up loud again so I could discover
how it was Eartha Kitt could deliver that song,

"Under the Bridges of Paris," so sublime, where the young lovers
turned & they fell into imponderable, immeasurable knots of love

with one another & I saw *me,* under the bridges too, announcing myself
to *her*—my wife—so that we could live in that excited, animated firing

that a brain, deep in love, can accomplish when it hurls itself
against all the loneliness—inside the insanity of deep hearted wishes—

& out here today, just sitting alone on this park bench,
every hour of that night, long ago, blinks & flutters here before me

like a calendar of tiny, lost, tormented softcover memories . . .

*

& maybe all human contemplation collects what's been held autogenic
in the thickness of the body. &, upon this recall, all the old memories

collapse into a blue-feathered pile. *Blue feathers dropping on lace.*

I can't begin to describe it to you, beyond this set of colors. It just seems

like blue bird feathers falling, one at a time—into a creamy euphoria
    of lace. & maybe that's all memory is or becomes.

Except that maybe it's a cream-going-into-indigo, or a blueness of string
gradually tugged through a soft hole in the roof & then, into nothingness,

like a feverish string of insomniac stars strung down through eternity

so that when you try to locate it, later, all that's left of it is a distaste,
something avowed & admitted & yet, somehow echoic, & yet not at all

forgettable &, even then, inspective & heedful, attentive, like dust,
or a glimpse of a pre-dawn dream, floating random & imponderable.

& maybe this is what memory *sounds* like: like a fanning of bird wings
with bullets shooting through them so that, in their echo, one just hears

a repetitive whacking & flapping of wings, followed by an emptiness.

An empty illiteracy that mimics the silence of blue feathers dropping
   on cream lace. I can't describe it any other way. It's just this.

& once, I sat straight up in the front seat of my car & I bellowed out,
with Gladys Knight & The Pips, to "Midnight Train to Georgia,"

just to feel it, that galvanic, inflammatory willingness to ride something
far out of a comfort range & to fail at it, anyway & completely,

but that was a long time ago, before I was here in this luminous park.

& it was before I heard the whack-whack of bullets through feathers.
& the sudden, fog-cloud of nothingness where everything fails,
   & even
the almond blossoms we waded through, like a twilight path, vanished,
& the blue feathers fell, like illiterate memories, onto lace.

  But it's okay. It's alright.
I'm just sitting here on this little bench, sipping my whiskey
while the kids across from me discover the adventures inside twilight
   monkey bars—all the worlds they can climb into—
while their mothers' chitter-chatter on cell phones & sip tea.

*

& on the sonic transistor radio I discover, just now, Mr. Al Jolson,
blurting out "Me & My Shadow." & I am in another hotel room again,

& this time so sanctified I can't remember how it is I've even arrived
here; & I am struggling just to stretch the bowtie around my collar,

so as to tie it for the wedding I am in. & my legs shake a bit,
they tremble under me, & my leather shoes, supposedly steady—

    just a groom's pair, waiting to walk up to meet his bride—

slide left & right as I try to stand, watching myself in a small oval mirror
. . . just trying to find what it is I am so afraid of. So galvanized in.

& time is anomalous, it's a nomology of scriptures & edicts
we remember of ourselves—all the good & bad memories mind you—

    & all the memories that torment us or uplift us again,

& on this park bench, today, as the simple white clouds pass me by,
I forgive every moment I was mutinous & against myself because

I couldn't hear, or didn't even try to see the concluding bagpiper there,
standing listless & readied by the park gate, piping out that final song
    we'll all hear . . .

& to tell you the truth, he was always playing it, just for her & me.

& if I stop now & I wait, trying to end this poem, all I can hear—
as she & I dance under the apricot trees in this ephemeral park

while trying to recall the fragrant, nowhere smells of that day—
is Peggy Lee singing that song, "Mr. Wonderful;" & by God,

she's humming it; & she's humming it right on time, for me.

The Light Most Glad of All

". . . but home is the form of the dream & not the dream"

—Larry Levis, *Our Sister of Perfect Solitude*

Our Lady of the Rosary

Bring her in I say. It is nearing rush hour
and the sunset along Woodward Avenue
melts into nasturtium yellow down I-94.
I have been drinking at a lonesome bar
where a Vietnam Veteran, searching
for porn on a small computer, has broken
into chrysanthemum tears over the loveliness
of a woman's thighs. I have left there
and walked up into this church to silence
my mind of rumination and trouble.
And so the priest brings her in. She seats
herself in a swarm of light that resembles
flowering kale and swimming mackerel.
The light funnels through the rose window.
A small fly trying to escape tortures itself
against glass. The priest hands me a black rosary.
We begin with the Sorrowful Mysteries.
It is not what I expect. She tells me this is for
the end of your life. Asks me what I have done
with Desire. I answer it is a fish I have chased.
Asks me should I ever catch it. I answer
it is not catchable. Mackerel swarm around
the shape of her body. My hands quiver.
Become fish. She asks if I have committed
Avarice. I answer the shape of a woman
has changed the way my eyes see and so yes.
I say that Avarice is just the confusion
of the flesh against the Ineffable, and so *yes*.
I have committed Avarice all my life.
I have chased the shape of a woman
through my pupils all of my life. *Yes.* I've
confused her with the Ineffable falling apart.
The priest moves nervously in his seat.
She asks me to speak of the Crucifixion.
It is the hill on which the Ineffable
and Avarice pray, I say. And we spend
our youth running into it, confusing it
with suffering, with clinical depression,

with all manner of pharmaceutical remedy.
The halo of thorns has hummingbirds
surrounding the head. They are sins.
Also they are the prayers we pray ecstatically.
In the end they are the Holy Spirit in us.
The wood of the cross is the skeleton.
The storm on the hill is substance *into* spirit.
The hummingbirds are the marvelous,
which is why Avarice and the Ineffable
are the beads we pray along the body rosary.
We pray inside Avarice and Ineffability.
Confuse it with joy, with our suffering.
She waves her hand at me. She stirs
the fish through her silver luminosity
so that they resemble aubergine petals.
Tells me the Ineffable is the holy smoke
inside loving. Breathe it in to yourself.

The Archangel Jophiel, Laying Down on the Blanket w/Me

(after Lee Young Lee)

The real apocalypse will be internal, she says.

It will be the inside fire that ultimately frees us.
The capillaries in each arm, the cells in each one, a lit flame.

I'm laying here beside her.
We're at this lovely picnic.

A bottle of champagne between us.

She's a cluster of salt and flowers. It's so hard to see her.

In the orchard's cathedral aisle of flowering almond trees,
mysterious birds keep landing and hiding in the branches.

Sometimes, down a row, a whole canopy will drop white blossoms,
then sweep them back to source. She leans into me, whispers:

You'll think each cell in you is a good deed—
offerings, tithing, or lovely moments of being authentic.

You'll even have memories of those good Samaritan acts when
you picked a hitchhiker up, or served soup at the soup kitchen,
or fed the orphan child a spoonful of oatmeal.

Even kissed your lovers, each one on the mouth, with rose petals.
Made good on all your promises. Accrued no debts. And then she says:

We mustn't ever confuse good deeds with the second soul,
the phantom carriage. She says this to me, straight to my face.

Pulls a strand of hair across her forehead, up, over it.
Adjusts the small golden hoop earrings again.

I can make out, in the spring light's glare,
her mouth, speaking cleanly, annunciating.

Your mouth, I tell her, resembles a Santa Rosa Plum.
I lift a hand up to touch her lips.

She fusses me away.

Her offending hand, ringed, like my wife's hand.

Each hour you pray is a spirit fire, a torch for the other truer self,
she says. The cells and the nucleus lit up, bird of paradise flames.

You *make* the soul-double—it's a horse and carriage—the dreaming
body.

Even the factions of angels blowing their wild-hearted
trumpets and howling out at the universe on their golden saxophones

won't join the dreaming body when it lets go of its heavy load
and it travels, a spear or a lance, to its first and utmost true source.

The first and last intent of *spirit*—of that multiphrenia within the
body's atoms, of the golden somersault—is *expansion*. And then

the intent reaches a turning point. It abandons even what carries it.
What happens, after that, is what waking from the dream is made of.

Good deeds, to be sure, she said—well, they pleasure the body's atoms.

What about the theatrical angels, crouched in the hallowed hulks of cars?
What are they, to me? I ask her.

They seem to live in a fluctuating state of harmony—I say—
like fractured shards, like minerals. Like prayer beads.

Oh, the quirky angels, she says . . . go ahead, enjoy every one of them
. . . even me . . . we are fragments and splinters of your dreaming light.

We strengthen, like a million atoms, in your temporary body . . .

Any visitation from us is meant to show you a single part
of what you truly are . . . your fantastical nature, good or evil . . .

That is always their one good, useful trick. They assist.
Now, she rises up on her left arm. Looks square into me:

Once you witnessed this at a carnival. You watched yourself
squiggle like a shrinking, wiggling gnome in the carnival's

crooked mirror. The girl beside you, her blond hair suddenly
rising like a hurricane of yellow straw from her head

and her amorous mouth—snaking across her reflected

recollected face—you saw that, didn't you?—her mouth,
like a stripe of maraschino cherries, blushed, so red.

Do you recall what you saw there? She inquires.

I roll over, across the flower-covered blanket to answer.
Look direct into her Cobalt blue eyes, answer:

I saw her young alive smiling face. And I saw it
drowned in pure cornflower blue, I swear to you I did.

I saw that she and I blurred into one another . . .
until we were a full totality. Butterscotch. Maize. Lemon.

You resembled then two spreading lemons? she asks.
You were hypnotized together, yes? Is that what you saw?
Yes, I say. Two lemons. Merged. No boundary there.

And then what? the picnic companion asks me.

Well then—I say—
Then, I pulled her by her hand, and we ran out of the Tunnel of Love . . .

and in the wild grasses—behind a large convoy truck where
the juggler, slowly getting drunk, spied on us and, along with

the trapeze swinger, the two of them playing gin rummy at a side table
as they lazily waved as we passed them by—right back there

we lay together, she and I, under a tree, and we kissed. Yes, that's
exactly what happened. We kissed until we were sleepy, I say.

Love: the hypnotic auric field, she says. Rest your memory there.

Love's an hypnotic field. An opened crack in this broken world.

And the real apocalypse will be internal. Remember this.

To satisfy its wish—this phantom Immortal body I speak of—
is to know that the body, right here—the *you*—is just an emptiness.

It's meant to invite in this other light: this dream, this Immortality.

She rubs her breastbone. Under her dress. There.
The other side always gathers back its light. Its immortality.

I lean closer to her.
Try to find her cheeks, her lips, her blinking eyes.

The sunlight, slanting and bursting lemon yellow light
through the clouds, blazes on her. She adjusts her sunglasses.

I can't quite recognize her face. She's glistens like a salt bed.

I roll over, run my fingers across the sand slopes of her arms.
Whisper that the light across her cheeks, her lips, is divinity.

Call her Murmuring Eyelashes; call her The Tangle of a Dream.

Love's an ideogram of the Immortal, she intones, arms behind her neck.

That's why love lays naked and bare all the deceiving images
we seem to venerate so much. It's an illusion-buster, Love.
It's a reflection with no inherent images. We see only what we *give* to it.

She rolls over on her belly. Takes a sip of the champagne.

Fusses with her hair, her pearls. Runs her finger across her left wrist.
She says: Love's *intolerance*—its slap in the face, its tempestuous
nature—is what brings us to a second level mindfulness. Which is *faith*.
We must slow down to know the deeper worlds within us. That hot
loneliness, so full with atmosphere; that bright deliverance, in light.

Endurance, tolerance, these aren't quite the correct words for faith's
power.

Faith, dear boy, she says to me, is seeing the possible within the *actual*;
it's not like hope—which gazes into the possible; inhabits the creative
spark there. Lights the spark-flame. But faith . . .
Faith is a telescope: it sees the *shape,* the *one,* with the zero inside it.

We need enough faith to contain what hope provides to us, she says.

Closer in resemblance to faith is the word, *align.*
Do you know, that from the Middle English, it means "Copulate?"

Now I caresses her clavicle. Now she opens up her throat, sighs.

Align:
to store data in a way that builds consistency into memory's architecture.
Go ahead—she says—look it up: on that computer you use to acquire
your knowledge.

Align, you know, meaning, can I stay with you for a sequence
of sun-drenched days. Can I earn the bounty of being there?
Align, meaning to marry, like a *betrothal.* Like a tethering to the atrium,
apse and chancel of our lonely body. To get absolutely lost in the breeze's
un-ripened empty glow . . . the dream's wistful nuptial . . . its vagabond,
bohemian elegance . . . to cross all the voids . . . to find another's light.

The lovers, chasing each other's love song. *Obsession. Fixation.*
Well, *Desire*—by any other name, she says. Rolls over to me.
Eyes on me. Says:

Savor in it. Bask in it. Run your curious fingers through the sensation
of it. Hold your wife's face to yours; and luxuriate in the perfume of your
wife's skin. Its youthful glow. All the rose blossoms in her cheeks.

Marvel at the way that memory is the universe that re-tastes the eternal
within it. Marvel at how the Eternal Gazer in you records the code.

It's so magical, it's so delightful, this dream, she says. Smiles.

The girl at the carnival was a flame-shaped angel. An apparition.
She cannot ever be touched by you again. She's luminous essence.

The Italian woman at the punk show: she's smaller than a caraway seed
now. You couldn't find her in a bowl of simple soup.

The bride you married behind the bag pipes: she's just a delighted dream
now. She's running away from you, over stone steps in her sun dress.
She's just fleeting white flower petals inside a rain that scatters.

It's only a past that chases a rucksack of retreating apparitions.

Rolls over, says to me: The past . . . a stuffed, unassailable wind.
Songs and words. Song and dance. It's so wistful, it's so alone.

The fire—our Spirit—thus becomes the prophet. It can't be disputed.

Smiles alone at this. Waves a small fly away from her tranquil face.

What abides in faith is what the curious hand turns over and over;—

it's some mystery that only tomorrow morning's dreams are made of;—

and that's a private riddle given to us by a personal answer that only we
can ever truly question . . . alone, in our private light, on a hillside.

Runs her finger gently over her top lip where the V of her cupid's bow is as she whispers this to me. Her cupid's bow, pink like a dip, slipped into a woman's grin. The dip in the lip like the V of a vagina. All is woman.

And sometimes it takes a lifetime to get the true answer . . . matched . . . inside the true original question. Sometimes many lives, she says.

Smiles again at this. Knowing the Immortal way. The familiar puzzle to solve.

Knowing too that our lifetimes are like a deck of cards tossed high up—

falling down to the ground in a clutter. A dragon fly there. So irrepressible.

That the shining thing is the immediate thing we always run to. That temptation, you know, sometimes keeps us at the party way too long.

So it is, she says.

She lays back, speaks the rest of this to a bird in the sky, says:

Knowing too, that the irrepressible *is* the attraction. The end point.

It is the fire inside us—that deep need in us—that we always run to.

Knowing too, that the savoring of the touch, of the first moist kiss,

of the two monogamous fingers held so romantically entwined as one,

is the epilogue of the last chapter, it is the final curtain, the picture

in a frame that holds us . . . until atrocity's maiden, its bloodthirsty messenger—this life's strange if allotted benevolent companion

completing its harrowing voyage up from the stream bed like a garrulous fish with a lion's torn mouth—

comes right for us with its rabid taste for survival. She blinks at the sky.

Knowing all this,

she continues,

means that you take the savoring and you melt it in your mouth:

the taste of the world *is* what memorializes us in the Immortal.

You're not ever just the hotel space of a physical body, she says to me.
You're what death does, when it broom-sweeps the almond petals
into two crisscrossing gold beams . . . into Life and Light. *Creation.*

And then, to spin them into a life . . . is to become the wedded one.

Every spark of light implodes / explodes: these are the almond petals,
crystallized divine, she says. The Gazer liberates into pure light.

And your warm light *is* the answer that love gives, to the first question—
which is what one must *do* with one's body.

Which is to admit into it a light most glad of all: an image of eternity.
All this delighted-light experience. Yes. Brushes her hair aside.

And it is a tenderness inside that eliminates all the territories, out / in.
Love admits, she whispers. And the out / in *dissolves,* makes peace.

I move closer to her. Watch how she rolls her auburn hair in between
her ringed fingers. Watch her rub the blue veins on her left wrist.

She rests her forehead on mine. Says, go ahead, *gaze into me.* I know you
want to.

The real apocalypse, she says, is always internal. It is in us.
The spirit frees itself inside love . . . And love . . . well it's so *infidel* . . .

Love's just a vehicle to the higher, remote light. The Immortal light.
Love's Gazer . . . is just one of the perceivers that guides you there.

The bird she's been following hang-glides and it flies way up
into the uppermost trees. It parachutes into a nest.
It disappears from view. A small fist of clouds moves across the sun.

She lifts her skirt up now to her knees. Winks at me.
She brushes off the flowers. Yawns into tranquility.

Says to me: it is an unbendable spiritual will that is served by the greater
light in us. Opens my shirt. Tickles my chest. Holds my chin. Says:
It is a deafness, and a crying deep in us that warns us we will be seized
by the alluring, faceless Spirit of this world. We hear it or we don't.

Yes, tangle of the dream, I say. *Yes, Light Infused in My Heart. Yes,
Field That Harvests all the Rules of the Day,* I say.

We feel its light upon us. That's *Source,* shivering us awake.
We must tolerate it—in order to be challenged by it
and indeed to be loved, to be saved inside it, she says.

And she runs her fingers across her eye lids. Sighs.
Fixes a gaze on her toes. Stretches them back. Wiggles them out.

And it's a book that glows like a bright light in the Dream for us:
Its pages spinning, turning; it's always here. Yes . . . I say . . .

Yes, Moon Glow, yes Salt-Love My Love All Over the Scars
of the Earth, I answer . . . Yes, days that wood smoke into rivers.

Do you think it teaches us
a true patience toward the unknown? She asks.

Fusses with a small clump of dust on her finger. Does it arrange mystery?

Yes, I answer: It teaches us—one by one—
to roam—indeed to roam—inside *all* the fields of memory; of mystery:

And . . . to be possessed by a *lie* . . . until we long for an answer—
some submerged, forgotten, ephemeral sacramental yearning
we perceive as *the answer* that prefigures *all* eternity—and I say:

that must be the sense of the many, *already in us,* which is love.

Yes, she demurs: the law *rebels* against the law until a stone turns,
it twists like a bright gold clock down into sand,

and the eyes of love—like awakened orbs, like lilies lit in darkness—
enlighten the soul. The servant knows all this, she says.

It speaks that we would understand it. The voice of the speaker,
the beloved—she says—*is* the fabric, listening-speaking
from the Eternal world. Below us. Above. Do you hear me? She asks.

I hold her right foot in my hand. *I speak memory to all names,* I say.

And she says: *By prayers of sorrow desire yearning and calling
to the beloved, we are taught a true patience of knowing.
It teaches us a renewable trust—which is a prefiguration
to all our freedom.* Then she moves over, looks into my face, says:

Trust that the One Law always rebels against the Other Law until the
incommunicable world that was once a terrible un-living

becomes ripened: it's a whirlpool of one soul meeting itself in another.
And to follow it—always—is what we all come here to do.
Or else, why bother living? Why suffer if not to know this opening?

Why not make the impossible possible? . . .
Life & Death dance in the gooseflesh.

The Gazer liberates.

And that is this elucidated beauty . . . the you, the her, all these past lives. The wandering vagabond in you that gives all his namesakes away . . . back into the Cosmos. The book that writes the code into timeless din.

To awaken from the coma of one's self. And to be *in* the opened space. And to see . . . and to know who will be standing there / alongside you for a brief intimate spell / for a cadence of radiant days / until light's end.

To find the One true love that will teach you all the meanings of love. And to know joy in one's abundance; enlightenment in one's poverty.

———

This was in the almond groves—in the San Joaquin Valley—

where the fragrant blossoms fell from the almond branches

like frosted fragments of artic white snow, like bridal flora,

and the remains of my body lost consciousness for a while

like I was laying in a soft-feathered bed of swollen swan's feathers—

almond blossom flowers—until she roused me awake again,

whispering to me—not yet, the light's gladness isn't quite ready

for you yet. It waits. *It will go on loving by eternal light. And far off*

I could smell the sweet aromas: Perfumed skin; a scent of honey;

and I could hear a lone field worker; a migrant: he was singing

a lullaby about a lake of swans, and that there was a girl and a boy

walking beside it, trying to remember what part of the road back

to town they'd have to walk—it was all through the erotic orchards—

just to get themselves back home for dinner, for some sleep time;

and that the most substantial part is what you come back here

to find, the Angel . . . whispered / whispers . . . to me . . . that's it;

that's all it ever was here or ever will be; that's it, that's all, she said.

Now I pull myself up to see her. The sunset blinds me, it dazzles me, but I see her in her sun dress, running through the almond tree lanes.

The evening shade—under the almond trees—explodes her into a star of fragrant white blossoms. To original pieces of the starlight orb.

———

The wind brooms her into a corolla of petals. That's it. That's all.

And the mystery spins her into silence. Spirals her image away.

One Holy Night, Santa Fe, New Mexico

We were laying still on a bed. Years into our journey.
She whispered to me that her hands were aging
quicker than mine. *Look at the purple veins.*
Preposterous, I argued. Her slender fingers,
like pink penstemon, like Santa Fe phlox,
the arms like trail head stems, like finely divided yarrow.
Do you think we will remember one another
after the rainstorm, the hurling thunder?
After the light flickers out in the lantern. . .?
she asked me, the full moon, naked in the window.
On the side table, a bottle of red mesa wine
& a sky thick with stars the color of yucca, mariola,
& dark too, as someone's secret.
Maybe we will die & be reborn here, she said.
On One Holy Night, I whispered to her, we will.
& over there—where the river softens, it widens,
it trickles, laughs and wiggles into emptiness
&, under the stone bridge there, where someone's
dropped an old bouquet of flung flowers
& where, up the road, behind a fence a solitary
guitarist strums curtains away for doorways—we will
find someone, an old person, sweeping away
the almond blossoms from a floor. Yes we will.
& inside the blossoms, there will be cut paper.
We will find one another there. *Two names.*
& over here, where the Dutch linen shirt
hangs like cream . . . & the boot heel scuffs of night
form into a little rooms, into narrow windows,
I will find you as the rain funnels a road to mud.
I don't *think* you into tomorrow, she said.
It is only a feeling, deep in there, where black sticks
scatter into a crust of ravens . . . & a woman strolls
past a window, she looks into it, she recognizes
a book on a shelf with a photograph
of an almond grove on it, & a man in a hat—
low to his eyes—watches her, looks away,

waits until the dusty velvet of night
tames a lullaby into Spanish & a parrot voice
chitters & it chatters in the exact way
that memory does when it is a sharpened knife,
when it insists, like we do, to come back. . .
this is what I see when I see you & I, she said.
I remember the way you looked into me
in Paris, in Amsterdam, in Iowa, in Detroit
she suddenly said to me, eyes like blue blue iris
& . . . each night you were asleep / I was certain
you were asleep when you dreamed me / &
when I dreamed you / too / & I was a word
with a big feeling that would slip right out . . .
& you would take it, like a pearl earring / &
place it right back on my ear lobe / on my spirit,
to make me real just as I made you real with a feather
& that is how we found one another / like this . . .
& Yes. It will be like that . . . if it is to be so,
I said to her. We will blink / blink / blink . . .
& stare into the eyes of saints until everything
is familiar again, as if previously lived, yes.
& you will wear a hat / low to brow / & be
just as you are tonight / eyes wet with tears /
& I will dab them / your tears / then wait, she said
until I can pronounce your name again / yes . . .
& I will watch as your stunned mouth narrows
like it is trying to suck on a hot chili pepper,
or re-taste my red lips on a napkin. & yes, you'll
wrap a vowel, a single word, an echo around
my name / like it is an embroidered altar cloth
& I will watch how a man—you—who never
talks to anybody, talks softly, in remembrance,
to me.

The Angel Ashriel Lifts Me Out of Me

At the bedside, I watch the slow pointillism
of the sunshine speckling the hospital walls.

Silence, and the hours like clicking trains.
Even my skin, a bitter orange, softens.

I am old now, so old the sky seems youthful.
My throat, bound by an old slingshot necklace.

Music, deep in my body's earnestness, echoes.
Visions, cut in purity, float up above the words.

The future was tossed over my bedside, and I saw how it is
I would vanish and die. *Loneliness,* whispered

the utopian nightingale angel to me—*that pining bird*—
is an impassioned utterance, reveling inside the day.

Caught there—my selfhood—in a swarming throe.
My shoulders and legs held tight, inside my arms.

Me, gazing into the volcano of a sunset's ending.
Love, you know—the nightingale angel said to me—

is a mode of virtual space; nothing but *life* contains it.
It resides in that lone part of the human—cut from the

floral rosette we like to refer to as the soul. Love—
the soul's laughing, tormenting, romantic soft ale—

is what the body longs to hold on to at the edge
of these late hours, on any lonesome day. And, so,

let me inform me of your future, said the angel,
lifting himself over the side of my bed's railing

to lay down with me like a salamander, so fused with me.
You will be the clearest bloom, drying up, shut.

And still, afterwards—when the uneasiness sets in—
you will be the crow's voice of a memory, recalling all this.

Yesterday, after roaming the queer, unnatural fields
where the old Victorian mansions fell apart

into the afternoon's ruinous bell pepper sunset
and, after a few stray feral cats leapt up to greet me

across the dappled wood planks scattered there
like squatter's quarters, I lay out along the dirtiest

portion of earth to experience how to give over,
to surrender, especially when everything else I saw

rose high up into the dusk's salmon truffle hue.
Radiance and strength, all the dancer's powers, so visible . . .

Nothing of it, when the funeral coal of dusk descends . . .
And laying there, thinking of that vision now, as

the shuttering of the day's last red flame grows stiller—
numbed with a carbonated glow of violet cobalt—

I am rendered formless in this magic oval, my body.
And the angel Ashriel—clinging to the sensual insides

of the room's soft draperies—waves hypnotic light
within the hospital room's sad gloomy cataract.

He arrives now to separate the soul from my body—
as if it were a bug just clinging there to the inner rails

of my rib cage. Something of me loves the world
as my body suffers. Some part of me, leaping, swirling,

parting and joining all over again, abides. My hands,
arms, tangled in confusion now as my body releases

its flung light. Hurls it like ginger ale into the space.
Love, the angel says, *must be consecrated by loss.*

And the light most glad of all must roam onward—
free to enter and depart the body, flinging images.

It is a shuddering, shaking immediacy, a pulse of life
intended for space and time, which is the mystery's

one sensory value: this illusion of a life whose events
I create. And I lose myself within this meaning—

so that I am abstracted from all sense of personal life.
I am a phantom flame, a single star exploding.

Just a hot orb of almond blossoms blown straight up
so that, at apex, I vanish into the night's crusade.

I empty out like a barn; just ghostly spider webs hanging.
I grow utterly silent: a theater stage without a soloist.

It goes on and on like this, like I am a pixilating orb—
and I resist it some more, run back to my breath.

The angel hovers alongside of me, a partner, an ally.
Something of me, concentrated in this particular act,

is unable to adjust. And the angel Ashriel—soft, furtive—
leans into the curve where my chest, stretched into

a shell of satin light, bulges out—widespread, bold—
and, as the starlight jiggles me, his small bony fingers,

old as ancient tree branches ground sharp to cartilage,
grip my soul, that rosette, and he lifts it away from me

so that I am drained like a thin stalk of all its light,
and my soul, a whorl of almond blossoms, is now his.

Something of the eyes, closing upon this torment.
Something of the heart, traversing its watery violet.

The Angel with a Winterberry in its Hand

The slender, elongated black branch, bleeding with winterberry.

I climbed up a patch of autumn weeds—up slope—to find it.
The red glowing berries, like *I love thee* on a lover's finger.

Then I crouched there, underneath the winterberry
as the whole sky above me swirled and tormented itself

with a winter snowstorm about to break open.

The blue lake below and the blue sky above me—china blue—
wearing the same exact face.

Love *finds* poverty, the rawboned angel-being said to me,
and when it finds it—someone's poverty—

the winterberries pulse red. The skies turn blue.

It torments even the satisfied among us.

~

What I remember the most is the exact way that her voice sounded

on the telephone
when we were confessing to each other
and how, in between her words, I'd hear my own poverty

filling in
all the spaces of the sensual silence.

~

In the silence poverty finds itself alive.
I thought it was the reverse: that love would quell poverty.

When we'd hang up I'd watch my fingers still holding the phone.
My knuckles, reddened.

The inconspicuous white flowers in a vase, there on a table.
Something of her face, shadowing in the windowpane.

That the lover's image is always a quivering.
It's never solid.
And my poverty, like human desire itself, so unwavering.

Something of the winterberry angel already there.

The silences
in between every one of her words. In every whisper.

I thought they'd leave me be, I said aloud
to the red winterberry.

~

The winter skies hoisted up the entire meadow.
Cast it down again as snow.

~

Some other memory
now intruding upon me and the rawboned angel-being:

The winterberries that she and I held in our hands
one winter morning after we'd walked so silently—

after we'd walked
into our vastness,

the berries we held there, so red.

Her

You could paint her like Rilke, the angel said to me
in the slow crawl of the late afternoon's blistered heat

as the larger flowers / the lilies, / wilted / fell out
and the sparrows raided the sour, lazy fountain.

Don't you mean like Rothko? I asked, his reds / yellows
bordered by those massive charcoal black rectangles?

Something / in his work / suicidal . . . / like perhaps / by
being *out* of love / we'll become amorphous / inorganic /

and / the repetitive way we color *all* the feelings coming in / and
streaming out of us / like waves of blue time. Yes.

The light of the day / her face inside a frame / a picture frame /
something only I could retain until she left me / what? blind?

Is Love then / a sadness leaving the body? He asked.
No. Sadness comes back in rectangles of nostalgia . . . / I said.

But we resolved this, the angel stammered / then said.
We *resolved it* / just like the stars / over the cliff / shred themselves

to pieces . . . / just like the *self* / as *it* splinters into atoms / awakens . . .
Yes, I answered, we resolved it / just like a card game

where the dealer / cuts in / at any time / on any day /
throws an Ace / and / yes, I'd strip the mauve curtains

from that hotel we made love in / in Nova Scotia / yes /
and I'd paint her like Rilke / with those merciful angels

so desolate / so very eager / for form / oh yes / and in the purple
light of the dusk's moonshine / it's refuge years / its presence /

I'd paint her among the angels / the angels / leaning in
to smell her as she / combed her hair / alongside the one / dying

dogwood tree / . . . that one that we pulled / out of the lawn
one late summer's day / after it died / . . . just like a tree

of blooming moons / losing all its white light / . . . Yes / that's it! /
the angel said / You've got it / those moon flowers / dissipating

their light / that's it / . . . and that to paint her / just like Rilke /
is to paint her / oh so gently / so gently / her light / so divine.

The Light Most Glad of All

The tongue is carnival, is light of the most divine.
I'm thinking this as I cross the beach at Ocracoke.

The outer banks, North Carolina, all the spent shells
hurled up / pitched by waves / across the tawny sand.

The spent shells like formula sonnets we can / read.
Can curl up in our hands / and love / forever.

Am thinking how boys seek light / and girls / wear it /.
And that boys / in their light / become men

broken and re-assembled / from that light most
glad of all . . . / that women / . . . and a marriage / *keep*.

Betrothal being / like light itself: / the coupling
of color / and absence / or like two lemons on a shelf

I once gazed at / in their exact splendor / from Africa.
And that color's just the stock in trade of the light

most glad of all / seeking itself / by way of formula.
That love's a *trade-off* of what robes it / and what

disrobes it also . . . / so that nakedness / is the light most
glad of all. Am thinking the light most glad of all

is what my wife smiles / when she's finding me
in that old darkness . . . / am thinking once I held her

after a nightmare . . . / this was in Paris . . . / odd light
crossing the weary hotel walls / and cockles

resembling the very same shells / in Ocracoke
and that / as we woke up together / we cried

from inside the light most glad of all. She's not
who this poem's about / but lovemaking / is / the

light most glad of all / surfing our bodies / for
resemblance / for that luminous / afterglow / for

that range of cockle shells our bodies are made of
when we lay there / moon struck by grief, / by

that strange tranquility that seems to shadow us / like
silk / when we hold one another / in love / in hurt

in gratitude / in fear / in that *afterwards*. And /
when we walked the Paris streets we were

washed by the late afternoon sunlight at a café
where an old couple gently held hands / him

wrinkled like / an old newspaper / and her /
onion-skinned and perfumed / like violet /.

And that Olivier Messiaen / from the light most
glad of all / wove the strobe lights of the eternal

as he crafted song from the light of birds / while
imprisoned by German soldiers / so stiffened up

by their falling away from music / from peace / . . .
and that Messiaen / could feel it / their hollow

ignorance . . . / and to offer them something / he
gave them streaming life / surrendering itself

not to death / not to nation or to state but /
in fact / to / that light most glad of all / yes.

And I'm thinking of that old couple in Paris.
How they seemed / what? / untroubled / tranquil /

as if they'd surrendered / long ago / to something
not made of bone but / rather / of lemon—

like sunset / like dawn / like the way / skin
softly shimmers / under dawn's / instrument.

And that as they spoke / I could see lemon
light / negotiating time / and distance / in them.

That the world of the light most glad of all / is / well /
angels / merciful intercessory / visitors / *near* us.

That the world's tempest is the light most glad
of all / stripping us / of unrest / into tranquility.

And that Baudelaire / that angel / bringing his
halos drawn of pure light / *knew them* / in *us* / . . .

that old couple . . . / in that café in Paris . . . / so made
now of lemon light / streaming up / awake.

And he found us / exchanging our light / from
that light most glad of all / like it always / in us / *is*.

Coda: Afterwards

You were sitting in meditation again, awake with all the deities
around you. You were outside of all religion. Totally free of it.
You were in the intermediate stream of the light most glad of all.
& the small lamp burned there, glowing like forbidden tattoo
so that all the darkness, surrounding it, seemed like skin,
& your folded legs, heavy as fresh baked bread, ached,
& your mind—so empty if felt like a dark oven, a bowl—
was more wide than a case-bound book, emptied of words.
All the visitors—the Christian ones, the pagan & the Gnostic ones—
help one with just one thing, the silence said to me.
& what is that? I asked it. & it answered me: to let go of even
what assists us, right at the edge of the rim where the dove is,
& where the luminous field is. & the white sails, just left
of the pine trees in the park—faultless, immaculate, so free—
wove themselves through the green boughs & my hands,
bankrupt, reached for them, into them, like ghosted debris,
like herding goats whose bodies had been shred to simple clouds
or like a truant privation, trying one last time for the physical.
Something in us longs for the physical; another, to let go.
& down by the trail opening where she & I had walked,
lived together, & spoke of what the water does in all its
mad dissolving, I could see, deep in there, what love does
when it is no longer sorry, nor alone, nor even attached,
like a strung vine, to the hungry body. & the white sails
moved through the boughs, through my name, & through
the chateau that lets go, & I was invaluable then, & free—
& married to a namelessness that is a treasury that must
be opened, like an endless love letter, a synopsis, et al.,
& then be read & read & read until then even the synopsis
becomes the dream, & not even the dream at all.

About the Author

Ken Meisel is a poet and psychotherapist from the Detroit area. He is a 2012 Kresge Arts Literary Fellow, Pushcart Prize nominee, winner of the Liakoura Prize, and the author of nine poetry collections. His books include *Studies Inside the Consent of a Distance* (Kelsay Books, 2022), *Our Common Souls: New & Selected Poems of Detroit* (Blue Horse Press, 2020), *Mortal Lullabies* (FutureCycle Press, 2018), and *The Drunken Sweetheart at My Door* (FutureCycle Press, 2015). He has published poetry in *Rattle, Crab Creek Review, Concho River Review, San Pedro River Review, Rabid Oak, Muddy River Poetry Review, The MacGuffin, Lake Effect, Panoply: A Literary Zine, St. Katherine Review, I-70 Review, Trampoline,* and *Sheila-Na-Gig.*

www.ingramcontent.com/pod-product-compliance
Lightning Source LLC
Chambersburg PA
CBHW022014160426
43197CB00007B/428